COMPUTERS AND OLD ENGLISH CONCORDANCES

computers
and

old english concordances

edited by
ANGUS CAMERON
ROBERTA FRANK
JOHN LEYERLE

Published in association with
The Centre for Medieval Studies, University of Toronto
by University of Toronto Press

© University of Toronto Press 1970
printed in Canada by
University of Toronto Press
Toronto and Buffalo
ISBN 0-8020-4024-1

The Figure on the cover is the Wyrm from the Slab of Wamphrey

foreword

This volume is a record of what was said at the conference on 'Computers and Old English Concordances,' arranged by the Centre for Medieval Studies at the University of Toronto and held on the weekend of 21 and 22 March 1969. The sessions of the conference were recorded and transcribed from tapes; these transcriptions were then edited by the original speakers, who were asked to limit their alterations to minor changes so that the published proceedings would represent as nearly as possible what was said. Only the chairmen's explanatory remarks have been abbreviated.

We hope that, as well as being the record of an occasion, this volume will be of interest and use to all who are concerned with lexicography and the use of computers in the humanities. Although the specific subject of the conference was Old English, the proceedings do have a relevance to any application of computers to the study of language and literature. For this reason, the table of contents lists specifically all the major papers and reports and the discussion of them.

We wish to acknowledge the help of the Canada Council and Dr C. T. Bissell, the President of the University of Toronto, in financing the conference. The Foundation for Education and Social Development of Boston, Massachusetts, paid the travel expenses of two of the British participants.

We also wish to thank the many people who helped with the conference and proceedings: the members of the Conference committee: Professors L. K. Shook, A. G. Rigg, H. A. Roe, and B. S. Merrilees; Mr Walter Bak; Mrs S. K. Higgs; Mrs L. Wilding; as well as Mrs J. Brasier, Mrs W. G. Kingsmill, the staff of Hart House, and the University of Toronto Press.

A. C., R. F., J. L.

contents

list of participants

RICHARD W. BAILEY
Department of English, University of Michigan
WALTER BAK
Centre for Medieval Studies, University of Toronto
C. J. E. BALL
Lincoln College, Oxford
BETTY BANDEEN
Department of English, University of Western Ontario
L. MICHAEL BELL
Department of English, Pennsylvania State University
JESS B. BESSINGER, JR
Department of English, New York University
ANGUS CAMERON
Department of English, University College, University of Toronto
A. P. CAMPBELL
Department of English, University of Ottawa
MICHAEL J. CAPEK
Department of English, Princeton University
JOHN CHAMBERLIN
Centre for Medieval Studies, University of Toronto
COLIN CHASE
Centre for Medieval Studies, University of Toronto
PETER CLEMOES
Emmanuel College, Cambridge
ROWLAND L. COLLINS
Department of English, University of Rochester
J. E. CROSS
Department of English Language, University of Liverpool
LAURENCE A. CUMMINGS
Department of English, St. Jerome's College, University of Waterloo
R. MacG. DAWSON
Department of English, Dalhousie University
CHARLES DONAHUE
Department of English, Fordham University
PIERRE R. DUCRETET
Department of French, University College, University of Toronto
ROBERT T. FARRELL
Department of English, Cornell University
ROBERTA FRANK
Centre for Medieval Studies, University of Toronto
MILTON McC. GATCH
Department of English, University of Missouri
CARL HAMMER
Centre for Medieval Studies, University of Toronto

PETER HATCH
Centre for Medieval Studies, University of Toronto
CONSTANCE B. HIEATT
Department of English, University of Western Ontario
NEIL C. HULTIN
Department of English, University of Western Ontario
EDWARD B. IRVING, JR
Department of English, University of Pennsylvania
FREDERICK G. JONES
Department of English, State University of New York at Binghamton
HUGH T. KEENAN
Department of English, Georgia State College
DAVID KLAUSNER
Centre for Medieval Studies, University of Toronto
JOHN LEYERLE
Centre for Medieval Studies, University of Toronto
HARRY M. LOGAN
Department of English, University of Waterloo
BRIAN S. MERRILEES
Centre for Medieval Studies, University of Toronto
R. BRUCE MITCHELL
St. Edmund Hall, Oxford
IVON OWEN
Oxford University Press (Canada)
PAUL W. PILLSBURY
Department of English, Eastern Michigan University
JOHN C. POPE
Department of English, Yale University
JOHN REIDY
Department of English, University of Michigan
A. G. RIGG
Centre for Medieval Studies, University of Toronto
R. E. ROBERSON
Department of Computing and Data Processing,
State University of New York at Binghamton
FRED C. ROBINSON
Department of English, Stanford University
JAY L. ROBINSON
Department of English, University of Michigan
HAROLD A. ROE
Centre for Medieval Studies, University of Toronto
PETER ROOSEN-RUNGE
Department of Computer Science, University of Toronto

JAMES L. ROSIER
Department of English, University of Pennsylvania
L. K. SHOOK
Pontifical Institute for Mediaeval Studies
PHILIP H. SMITH, JR
Institute for Computer Research in the Humanities, New York University
E. G. STANLEY
Queen Mary College, University of London
VICTOR STRITE
Department of English, University of Missouri
RICHARD L. VENEZKY
Department of English, University of Wisconsin
JOHN F. VICKREY
Department of English, Lehigh University
WILLIAM WHALLON
Department of English, Michigan State University

COMPUTERS AND OLD ENGLISH CONCORDANCES

friday afternoon

WHAT COMPUTERS CAN DO IN THE HUMANITIES

CAMERON On behalf of the Centre for Medieval Studies at the University of Toronto
and the Pontifical Institute for Mediaeval Studies I want to welcome you
to Toronto and to this meeting. I am very pleased that so many of you
have been willing to come on rather short notice – some on extremely short
notice – and that so many people have been ready to give informal reports
on work they have in progress. This meeting has only been made possible
through the interest and good will of a large number of people, and I hope
that the talk which takes place will lead to further talk, and finally to action.

There are two main subjects for discussion, and these are separate, though
related to one another. The first is a review of the present state of work on
computer concordances of Old English texts. The second is an exploration
of the possibilities for beginning work on a large-scale Old English dictionary.

I myself expect to learn a great deal during these next two days. I bring
to this meeting a strong feeling that this is a good time for intensive work
on Old English texts, and an eagerness to help with it. I am only beginning
to master the intricacies of computer concordances, and I do not have a
comprehensive plan for a large dictionary up my sleeve. My own interest
in these matters comes from my work with N. R. Ker's *Catalogue of Manuscripts Containing Anglo-Saxon.*[1] It seems to me that this volume has been
of great help to Old English studies, and that it has contributed to the re-
awakened interest in the editing of Old English texts in the past few years.
Ker's *Catalogue* and P. H. Sawyer's recently published list of Anglo-Saxon
charters[2] give us a basis from which to work, readily accessible information
on a corpus of texts for which we can make concordances or dictionaries.

I offer the following as questions which I hope may be discussed.

On computer concordances and dictionaries:
What are the linguistic and literary uses for computer concordances?
Should concordances be attempted for single texts, for manuscripts, for
authors, for the whole corpus of Old English writings at once?
Are the formats of present computer concordance projects compatible, so
that their products can be combined or used in larger projects? Professor
Venezky has given considerable thought to this question and will be talking
on it tomorrow morning.
What kinds of texts should we base concordances on? On manuscript facsimiles as well as printed editions? If only on printed editions, what should
be done about the present variations in approaches to editing and accuracy?
Is a large scale Old English dictionary really wanted? How should it be
related to the other historical dictionaries of English?

---

1 N. R. Ker, *Catalogue of Manuscripts Containing Anglo-Saxon* (Oxford, 1957).
2 P. H. Sawyer, *Anglo-Saxon Charters: An Annotated List and Bibliography,* Royal
Historical Society Guides and Handbooks, 8 (London, 1968).

On practical matters:
Is it possible to set up a clearing house for concordance materials at one
university where all can have access to them?
What sort of committee structures will serve a concordance series and a
dictionary best?
Should meetings of this sort be held every few years to review work on the
concordances and the dictionary?
Where will money be found for such projects?

If answers come to even a few of these questions, then the meeting will be
a success.

I would like to turn over this afternoon's session to Father Shook of the
Pontifical Institute for Mediaeval Studies.
SHOOK Thank you very much. I will call on Professor Jess Bessinger, of the Department of English of New York University, to give his report. Professor
Bessinger's new *Concordance to Beowulf* [3] is here on my desk, and I want
to extend to him my congratulations on the appearance of this, which is
bound to be a landmark in this area.
BESSINGER Thank you, Father Shook. If that book is a landmark and not a stumbling
block, it will be because Dr Philip H. Smith, Jr, was the programmer and
much more than the programmer for it. And while we are dealing out credit
where credit is due, I am very sorry Dr C. C. Gotlieb is not here this afternoon, because it was a conversation about Old English and computers some
ten years ago that began my own modest ventures into this field. Kelly Gotlieb one day said, 'Why don't you keypunch some *Beowulf*?' and, while this
seemed madness, I couldn't think of a reason not to do it, so he had 616
lines keypunched for a start, and it all began that way. Thus it was really
Toronto and the computer lab here that began it; Kelly Gotlieb began it
and Philip Smith finished it.

I have the grave and embarrassing honour of speaking twice to you in two
days, saying something general about computers and literary studies today,
and something special about Old English concordances tomorrow. I am
more willing to speak in generalities today because there are many people
here who can speak of particulars better than I.

Everyone here, though, will agree that the problems and challenges that
we face in this new field of research are problems of power, problems of
money and power – almost the same things. Since today's computers are
so unwontedly powerful and can perform routine operations so much
faster than human beings can, they may save scholars vast amounts of

3   Jess B. Bessinger, Jr and Philip H. Smith Jr, *A Concordance to Beowulf* (Ithaca,
1969).

physical labour and perhaps even a little intellectual labour. The only real question is, can this power of theirs be used economically? Can we afford it?

Their dumbfounding capacity for rapid work is useless to the literary scholar until symbolic transformations have altered the scholar's text into the machine's characters; and at the end the machine's output must be interpreted by a scholar. The scholar's relevant work is not much reduced, though he may be spared some drudgery. The machine enables him to do more relevant work, that is all. But to exploit this new technology, the scholar must do more than adjust to new machines. He must adjust to new working conditions, to new committees and bureaucracies. To exploit his new capital, he must as it were form new corporations.

In the near future, he may need to form a consortium of linked corporation centres. Indeed he will probably need to consult a time-zone chart before putting to work his distant telephone-linked computers. Plugging in two computers makes them much more than twice as strong; but if an operator in Toronto uses a linkage of this kind, he will need to know the time in, say, California, where he may have available a few seconds of consortium-leased, phone-linked computer time at a cheaper rate after midnight. We are facing a new order of challenges and a new range of bureaucratic complexities in the new literary electronics.

It is probably time that we began to ask what kinds of corporate response are appropriate to the opportunity. This meeting will shortly involve itself in committee-making, and it will be found that some difficulties are caused by the speed of technological change.

Computerized research is both enlarged and limited by quick developments in all but immediately obsolescent new machines, machines that were not designed for literary research in the first place. We must simply adjust to this inconvenient fact. Present technological advances are part of an evolution that has only begun to touch literary scholarship, though of course the method of digital calculation itself is anything but new. After the abacus (still more widely used today than the electronic digital computer), the future began to rush at us with Pascal's gear-driven calculator, Jacquard's automated loom, Babbage's memory-equipped calculator, and Hollerith's census-recorder, all before 1900. The first electronic digital computer dates only from 1947, but we should note that the first computerized literary research began in 1949 – that is how quickly Father Roberto Busa and the IBM Corporation responded to the possibilities for computerizing the Thomistic Index.[4] Things have continued to move quickly. If for our ambitions it was the first step – from abacus to Busa – that counted, the second step was almost as momentous,

4 Roberto Busa, 'An Inventory of Fifteen Million Words,' *Literary Data Processing Conference Proceedings,* Jess B. Bessinger, Jr, Stephen M. Parrish, Harry F. Arader, eds. (New York, 1964), pp. 64-78.

namely the development of more efficient machines and of machine programming systems so economical that university courses in natural-language programming are now widely available for undergraduates, who can address the computer in their mother-tongue if this happens to be English. A decade ago all this would have been impossible to imagine, but we must begin nevertheless to plan together for the next unimaginable decade, with all its necessary and unavoidable waste. Perhaps we can begin to trim the waste a little.

It does not follow that a literary scholar need use computers for his literary research unless he is working with massive amounts of data, and then he has no choice; he must use them. Clerical slaves of the human kind are no longer cheap to hire, and electronic slave-machines are no longer quite so expensive. But handling projects of a middling size is still a puzzle, and perhaps explains why literary computistics are today such a flourishing activity, so full of experiment and promise. This may also explain, but not excuse, the fact that our various experiments have to date been so ill co-ordinated.

It may be well here to survey quickly some areas in which computers have successfully been used for literary research. It will be seen that the areas are very unlike each other. Of special interest to textual critics in Old English texts is the work being done in later periods involving collation and recension or textual restoration or stylistic analysis. One of the most promising of such projects is that by George Petty and William Gibson of New York, who have been collating six printed texts of Henry James' *Daisy Miller* from a single master computer tape. This may sound simple to do, but it was a brave thing to have tried and a masterly thing to have brought close to accomplishment. A further step in the same direction is the computistical genetic recension attempted by Jacques Froger; whatever else may be said about recension, it is almost surely better performed by machines than by people. Textual restoration is another matter, but even so, lacunae in the Dead Sea Scrolls have been restored by computers at Gallarate. The critical analysis of literary texts – I had better be specific and say the attempted quantification of stylistic criteria – has been accomplished in varying degrees of complication and success for texts as different as the letters of Paul, the poems and plays of Shakespeare and Racine, and the *Federalist Papers,* to name only a few examples.

We have in effect been asking the machine simple questions at great rates of speed. The time is close or already upon us when the machine will begin to question us, at the same rates. For example, if a computer is given different contextual lists from *Beowulf* and told to make a composite list of formulaic matter in the poem, it will produce what is asked for. That is, it will bring together, conveniently, for the student to analyze, all strings of identical characters and spaces within certain measurements. We excitedly printed a sample concordance of this kind in the Cornell *Beowulf.* It will be noticed, however, that the machine will produce different formulaic lists when asked for different formulaic contexts: a 720-formula poem for a twelve-character context of identity, perhaps an 820-formula poem for a ten-character context of identity, and so on. That is to say, the machine compels its programmers to define their formular criteria more accurately than they perhaps want to. In effect, the machine raises questions about quantitative measurements of style. It is now asking us questions.

We should not fear these developments – a computer's activity is creative only by metaphor, since everything that comes out of it must be programmed into it. It is again only the rates of acceleration in computistic research that need concern us. In mere indexing alone, the acceleration suggests something about future prospects. For the Cornell series, the concording of Arnold required, I am told, about thirty-eight hours of machine-time, that of Yeats, however, only about twelve hours, that of Emily Dickinson only about ten hours, all on the same machine, the IBM 704. The later Blake concordance, with significantly more data but on a better machine, required less than three hours. Routine programming brings drastically improved efficiency. The exhaustive procedures by which machines automatically compile indexes of many kinds are as useful as they are now routine, but we have far to go in adjusting related procedures to these time-saving programs. The computer-generated concordance to *Beowulf* was compiled and sorted in little more than an hour of mere machine time, after which the book itself required more than two years of ordinary human time for publication. There is a generation gap here in which we are all destined to languish for a while yet. It is not the fault of the computers, which are improving faster than we can keep up with them. Allow me to cite further examples which must run the risk of sounding ungrateful or pessimistic, though I do not intend them that way.

The appearance of computer printout in its raw state does not flatter humanistic sensibilities, and of course was never intended to. The automated tabulating facilities of the earlier computers were used, because they were available, to make simple, sometimes almost illegible, indexes of standard literary texts. Only standardized texts can economically be indexed by machines at present, at least without lavish expenditures of pre-mechanical editorial time. The early machines were primitive as typographical devices, and the reproduction of their printout by photo-offset did little to improve appearances and much to obscure communication. Happily, improved formats are now becoming available in automated photo-composition. Photo-composed pages can look very handsome indeed – so much so that, I think, their appearance makes a quantum difference in the usefulness and longevity of the book.

The processing of non-standardized orthographies, however, a subject of painful interest especially to Old English specialists, will plague us longer than the appearance of Old English pages. As Kottler and Markman found in preparing their *Concordance to Five Middle English Poems*, the unstandardized orthography of old manuscripts may demand a formidable amount of editorial interference with the computer's activities.[5] These scholars resorted to manual editing for much lexical rearrangement even as more efficient machines appeared, to which it was not economical to transfer their project. The Old English poetic concordance project, too, has watched three technologies come and go. Tomorrow Professor Pillsbury will describe a pre-editing system for Old English texts that has won my deep admiration, except that it multiplies several times the scribal labour required to write the original manuscripts, before the computer stage is reached.

One may detect two possibly related morals here. First, the availability of certain machines governs what an editor-programmer tries to do with computerizable texts, and may explain why there have been more computer projects than computer publications. Second, the programmer-editor's sagacity involves more than knowledge of text and machine; he must know when to intervene in the interest of either. This will be true of all texts except those in a regular orthography; it will thus be true of all Old English texts except those normalized for special reasons. For a time we shall doubtless continue to co-operate with the machines by bending to their needs in order to exploit them better.

One way to do this is to improve communications within our own community. A single powerful computer, or linkage of computers, can do more than ten ordinary unlinked machines, and not ten times more but thousands of times more, if interchangeable programs are developed so that all workers in Old English are using compatible and converging programs. But in Old English research today a dozen researchers are using mutually unintelligible computer programs. We should all gain from a centralized international committee, planned facilities for the whole Old English corpus, standardized programming, and the exchange of tapes and other storage media. I must not trespass on Professor Venezky's discussion, which we shall all soon be listening to; his proposal for an Old English materials centre for the computer processing of Old English texts is just the kind of thing I am talking about. He has an exciting model to discuss and to work toward. Models for this kind of activity already exist outside our discipline. We in Old English studies have been delinquent. The literary and linguistic computing centre in Cambridge, England, is one which has concentrated to very good effect on Middle High German projects, for example.

We are here chiefly to talk about computerized Old English lexicons. Computerized English-language research embraces more than concordance-making, while some machine concordances important for Old English lie outside our field. I want to discuss briefly Marvin Spevack's Shakespeare concordance and David Erdman's Blake concordance.

5   Barnet Kottler and Alan M. Markman, *A Concordance to Five Middle English Poems: Cleanness, St. Erkenwald, Sir Gawain and the Green Knight, Patience, Pearl* (Pittsburgh, 1968).

A Complete and Systematic Concordance to the Works of Shakespeare,
6 vols. (Hildesheim, 1968-69) is based on the new Riverside Shakespeare
edited by G. Blakemore Evans and a distinguished editorial board. It is
designed as a set of interlocking concordances to individual plays, to
characters in the plays, to prose and verse in the plays, to the poems, and
so on finally to a merged concordance of the complete Shakespearean
vocabulary. Editors of copy-text and concordance worked together so that
the concordance lists a number of emendations to the copy-text. Here is a
new rule in electronic index-making. It goes beyond the rule put by Kottler
and Markman in their Middle English concordance, that ideally one should
have a concordance with which to make a concordance. Now one also needs
a concordance from which to prepare an edition from which to make a concordance.

David Erdman's *Concordance to the Writings of William Blake,* 2 vols.
(Ithaca, 1968), like the Shakespeare work, also concords a large corpus of
prose and verse, with expansions and emendations of the copy-text – the
Nonesuch Blake, the latest revision of which includes emendations based on
the first printouts of the concordance. Its production is as elegant as its process. As ambitious and even revolutionary as they are, the Shakespeare and
Blake concordances show computer-generated indexes at the top of their
present promise. Both were produced by corporations, that is to say teams
of scholars in trans-Atlantic co-operation. They make a mirror for our own
ambitions. No Old English projects of comparable scope have yet been
planned.

After linguistic indexes there should follow analyses of the language indexed.
In Old English studies, computational stylistics must wait upon the production
of the indexes, but there is reason to think that computerized analysis of
style – that is, of diction, syntax, and prosody – can be carried on for Old
English as it has been for later fields by Mosteller and Wallace, the Sedelows,
Clayton, Dearing, Raben, and many others. This work will be included within
the newest advances in computational linguistics, a field in which the machines
have already been most profitably exploited for models of generational grammar and for the beginnings of machine translation.

It is true that machine translation has to date seemed non-productive or
counter-productive from a literary point of view. Machines have proved
themselves only in the rough abstracting of documents; and yet grammatical
models for machine translation must of necessity teach researchers a great
deal about linguistic behaviour, and what is learned generally about linguistic
behaviour we shall later be able to refine in special studies, in Old English and
in other languages. Computer programmers have already accomplished translation of conventional printed English into raised-dot Braille coding, and in
this operation a very precise, if relatively limited, knowledge of linguistic
behaviour is required. For more subtle linguistic transformations to be made
by the computers, vastly more complicated grammars and vastly larger voca-

bularies must be accumulated. For Old English studies in this direction, data banks of the necessary size are not even to be contemplated as yet.

The Thomistic Index gathered by Father Busa and his colleagues can boast of the largest computerized corpus to date – more than ten million words. The next largest is closer to us, about five million words of Middle High German at Cambridge. There is of course nothing comparable for Old English. In Modern English, however, there is the exciting *Computational Analysis of Present-Day American English* by Henry Kučera and W. Nelson Francis (Providence, 1967), based on a computerized corpus of a million words – a mere million words! The basic taped records of this corpus are now being further analyzed in special research projects in America and abroad, while the printed volume itself is full of graphic suggestions for all students of English language and literature. It seems to show, for instance, what Old English scholars need to know as much as anyone, that purely quantitative measurements can be made of 'aesthetic' elements in language. That is, such measurements can be carried out mechanically if the corpus is large enough. Only a corpus which is machine-retrievable and adapted for magnetic-core storage will be large enough, and if we in Old English studies are ambitious enough to attempt such measurements we had best not leave the accumulation of a working corpus to random developments. If we can learn from computational linguistics how to change the level of our analysis of the Old English language, we shall be involved in a change as profound and creative as when biology or astronomy were transformed by modern scientific tools. The Kučera-Francis work, if I understand it correctly, opens the way to new avenues of research in the Old English lexicon.

Thank you for letting me speak so generally to you on these matters of special interest to us all.

SHOOK   I should like to ask Professor Ducretet of the Department of French, University College, to give his report. Professor Ducretet has done a concordance and index of Voltaire's *Candide,* and is working now on an index of Montaigne.

DUCRETET   May I first of all say that I concur with Professor Bessinger as to what computers can do. I have prepared something, however, of a much more practical and down-to-earth nature in order to relate to you some of the problems that are involved in the use of computers. I am afraid that perhaps I am being too fundamental, and that what I will say, you already know. However, I hope that for some of you it might be of some interest. I will also talk about some of the work that we have done here at the University of Toronto. It is rather small compared to that of the Cornell Concordance Series, but then we started a bit later, and maybe in the years to come something will be published of interest. And, of course, I will be speaking about French texts and not English texts, unfortunately; I wish I could.

First of all, I think that what should be kept in mind is that computers, as Professor Bessinger stated, do not replace men. In other words, there is no machine that has been invented yet that can think and has the potential of human beings. They, the computers, do not eliminate human errors. They do not think for themselves as some people seem to think, and they require manpower to function. What I mean by manpower is not only scholars who prepare the work and think of something that they want to do, but also manpower in the form of operators for these machines, of programmers, and of a variety of clerical help that one cannot do without. Unless one has this manpower, efforts are wasted to a great extent. This means that work that would take theoretically an hour on the computers might take six months. These are fundamental points that have to be kept in mind.

As has been said many times, computers have the advantage of doing things much faster than human beings, and this is why we are using them. They are an extension of human beings' senses. However, they need the reflection of human beings before they can be used. They are electro-mechanical and electronic devices and they are useless if they are not directed by man's intelligence and will. It's the same thing as for a car. No car is of any use if no one is driving it to any place, or if no one knows how to drive it. Using the computer is not an easy thing. It requires a means of communication; in the case of computers today, it is a language. One says that one can communicate with computers in natural languages. I am afraid that, unfortunately, it has not reached that stage yet. It is a natural language only in the sense that it is an organized language which you have to know, and if you make the least error the computer will not understand you. This language is put into the form of programs and you need someone to prepare this program, namely a programmer. That means communication between someone in the humanities, or in linguistics, or in history, as the case may be, and the programmer, who is mainly scientifically trained and who may not follow the path that your mind is taking. This of course creates a rather difficult problem to solve. A computer does not allow for human error. If your logic is faulty, the computer will incorporate all the errors that you have dictated to it. And it will repeat them hundreds of thousands of times whereas you might make that error once; so you have to be constantly on the lookout. This means an exercise in clear, logical, persistent thinking and planning, and in methodology, of course. One does not necessarily reach that stage on the first try. You may encode all of your information in a given way, process it through a computer, and then when you come to the results not get what you wanted. Somewhere along the line you forgot that it was necessary to encode another item which would have given you some sort of information that you found interesting. That means that from the outset you must know what you want as a finished product. Here, I believe, we are thinking of dictionaries for Old English, and, not being a lexicographer, I cannot envisage all of the problems there would be, but those of you who have dealt with lexicography know how complicated a problem it is. If you have to know beforehand all the entries that you are going to have to present to a computer in order to obtain a finished product, just imagine the complexity of the program and the steps you'll have to take. It's not an easy task by any means and certainly not a one-man affair.

Computers today are mainly scientifically and number-oriented machines. They are at the disposal more of people dealing with scientific, numerical problems than of people dealing with linguistic ones. And as a consequence you have either to modify the computers or make some sort of arrangement so that you may use them for language purposes. This poses a very serious problem, especially, as was pointed out, in the question of printing of material in a final format which will be in some sort of publishable form or actually ready for photo-processing. Because, if you don't have that, then indeed you must go again through a printer, and that means quite a bit of work, sometimes needless.

The next step is the problem of quantity. Most of the people in the sciences are concerned with the solution of a mathematical problem. This means a very small amount of information being presented to the computer, very complex programs which allow very long processing of the problem, and a very small output, sometimes a formula or a numerical answer. In the case of humanists, quantity becomes an enormous problem. If you have a text of a hundred thousand words, and I'm picking 100,000 as a small figure, and you have to process it, this means that you have, first of all, to prepare the text for key-punching, for punching on to cards, or on to tapes; then it means that these cards or these punched tapes have to be placed on magnetic tapes which will later on be processed by the computer. Now in order to run these cards or that information on to tape you need a certain amount of equipment, and more than anything, it takes quite a bit of time. And it is not easy. It sometimes happens that, in running 20,000 cards on to a tape, a job which takes five to ten hours, towards the end of the job, one or two cards will spindle and the whole thing will have to be started over again. It's a time-consuming affair.

Finally, there is the question of storing all of your information. I happened to be at the centre for computation at Besançon some years ago where they are working on French texts: they are putting them on to cards to prepare indices. A room about this size with shelves is full of cards, of boxes of cards; eventually the quantity of cards becomes so huge that unless you have storage room, you don't know what to do with these cards. You almost need a library just for cards. There is a problem of mass: you are producing with a very small text huge quantities of information on paper that you have to store and be able to retrieve when you need it. These are things that have to be considered. So what is the solution to that? I think that at this point there isn't any. Cards are still the best storage means, because tapes get erased and you cannot handle paper tapes because you cannot read what's on them: you'd have to interpret every perforation. As a result, you have to rely on cards to store and to prepare your data. If you think of a dictionary of a million words, you can start envisaging one million cards, one for each word plus the entries; you can imagine how many cards you are going to have to store somewhere. This, of course, implies the question of whether a centre for that sort of thing is not a better choice – a building which would be, let us say, fifteen stories high, with a basement maybe five stories deep, for the storage of cards. Furthermore, you have another problem that occurs and this is temperature. If you are storing tapes and the temperature is bad, your tapes just are ruined. As a consequence, you are right back where you started. If you have cards in a place which is humid, damp, or too hot, the cards start to deteriorate and when you try to pass them through the machine in order to put them on to tape and process them, you have one card out of two which spindles. Now I have done this mechanically myself and I assure you it is quite an irritation to spend whole evenings, and nights sometimes, just feeding the cards-to-tape machine, almost one card at a time. These things have to be considered. This also means that you need manpower, that is, someone who is qualified to do this work for you, if you can find such a person.

This leads then to the needs in hardware, as the word has become known, hardware meaning the mechanical machines or electronic machines or computers and others. What are the needs in hardware? Well, you need the information storage, you have the cards that you have to punch, so you need a keypuncher, and if you need a keypuncher, you need someone to operate a keypuncher. If you are going to punch one million words, I would like to know how much time this will take, no matter how good the operator is; I am thinking of a dictionary right now, more than anything else, since this was the purpose of this conference. Then you need a card-to-tape reader. You need to put these cards on to magnetic tapes, so that you will be able to process them by means of a computer. This means that you have to have a computer other than one of the large computers, otherwise it's much too expensive. Right now here at the University of Toronto we only have two 360s and one 7094, but we no longer have a 1460 which was a card-to-tape reader and tape-to-card reader or printer. As a consequence you have to do all of your manipulation through the 360 which is a very expensive machine to run, just to put cards on to tape.

About a week ago, I was talking with someone at the Library and they told me it took them three hours using the 360 to read six boxes, or 12,000 cards, on to a 360 tape drive, because there were a few little technical errors somewhere. I'm sorry for those people from IBM who might think that this is directed against them. It isn't. It's just fact.

Then you need a tape-to card reader which is again a 1460 or equivalent machine. Now the reason I'm saying you need this intermediate machine is that the work in the humanities is quantitative. If you use a computer of the order of the 7094 (that is the largest machine at present) or the 360, which are very fast processing machines, in order to go from cards to tape or from tape to cards, it takes a tremendous amount of machine time and it's very expensive. The order of cost for university usage is something like $350 an hour now and I believe that commercially it runs into the $700 to $800 an hour range. So you can imagine when you are dealing with huge quantities what sort of sum of money you are dealing with. If you lose one day or one run of four hours, that's $1,400 that you had to find somewhere. Allocations for that sort of work are very small, I assure you. I've been asking for money from the Canada Council, the University, and have begged and borrowed everything I could for the past five years, and it doesn't amount to much.

These are problems, of course, that you have. Then you need a printing system; that is, a tape-to-print system. Again, if you are printing through the 360 it is going to cost you a fortune and if you think of the output that you get from, let us say, a 100,000-word concordance, it just isn't printable. Not with a 360. You need some sort of machine which is inexpensive, perhaps slower, but that will allow you to print easily and to get your data on to tapes. This is a problem that has to be considered. The next step is that, of course, once you have a text that you have cut up into words, well, you need to add information for each one of these words, so that you must get a card for each word on which you will eventually add a lemma, in the case of regrouping problems, and encoding of some type if you are interested in semantic, stylistic, syntactic, or morphological analysis. This means that for a text you may have typed in a running format, you may have gotten 10,000 cards and you'll end up with 100,000 cards that are printed, but you have to get them printed from the tape on to cards. This means, again, hours of processing; if you do that through the 360, you'll never get the money for it anyway. It won't work! One has to be the Ford Foundation to be able to afford that sort of thing. Unless you do this type of work with some other sort of equipment other than a 7094 or a 360, it's *extremely* dear.

Then let us say that you are interested in this kind of analysis; I think that this is an important aspect that has not been covered by most concordances and indices that have been published so far – there are no tables or general graphs, plotted graphs, of the content and the results of text analysis, that is to say, synthesis of the quantitative analysis that has gone on. For instance, how many nouns are there in chapter one? For a work of thirty chapters, as I had with *Candide,* I would like to have a graph that would have come through telling me how many nouns there were, how many nouns before adjectives or after adjectives, depending on the case. I had all this encoded on my cards, but of course I need a program for that. I also need a plotter, if I get the program, for these things to be done. So that means you have to have a plotter at your disposal.

Then, finally, you need a sorter, a sorting device which is manual because, in many instances, going through the computer for sorting is first of all very expensive and then, more than anything else, it means you have again to go from card to tape, from tape to processing, from tape to card, and then back to analysis. And this together with printing. These are huge quantities of paper as probably Professor Bessinger will bear me out.

Then there is, of course, the manipulation of information by means of the computer. This means mainly sorting, putting into alphabetical order, analyzing, deciding if you want to know, let us say, how many nouns there are in your context, or how many kinds of noun appear before an adjective and how many times an article appears in such and such a context. These are manipulations which are internal. In this case the large computers such as the 7094, once you have your data there, are excellent machines for that. They will do that in an hour indeed. But then they will have to bring back this information to you and then again you will have to manipulate it. So this has to be kept in mind. Usually the 7094, so far, has been the machine used in that respect, but from what I understand, support for the 7094 is sooner or later going to disappear.

What is happening in the case of the concordance programs that we have here in the University of Toronto? They were developed by Professor Glickman, and I helped in a way by getting some money and discussing with him the sorts of problems that we all had. These programs were written for the 1401 and the 7094. The 1401 and the 1460 types of computers that were here at the University have disappeared. The only ones left are the 360s and the 7094. This means that the programs that were written for the 1401 have to be re-written now for the 360, since eventually the 7094 will no longer be supported by IBM. Everything will be directed towards the new generation of computers and this is where the problem arises: most of the programmers no longer would want to work on Fortran programming. They are concerned with work on programs dealing with the 360 because this is the thing of the future and if they don't know that language, then they won't be able to get a position giving them better salaries. You are faced with that aspect also.

Passing from that problem, we have the printing problem which I have slightly dealt with. Printing is one of the largest problems in a computer centre, or complex. Right now here at the University the 360 and the 7094 are processing madly, but they are not printing anything, or anything isn't the word, they are not printing half of what they have to because they just cannot do it. The 360 cannot possibly give you an output equal to its speed of processing. So that again, you need some other stages in order to get your printouts. What good is it to have a lovely tape on which there is the concordance of some text that you've worked on for six months, a year – usually it takes three or four – and here you are with your lovely tape, but you cannot print it. It takes you a month, two months, three months, before you can get a printout. Problems of printing are vital, and if you are going into large production such as dictionaries, concordances of large works, unless you have a centre behind you where you have all the facilities, and all the time needed made available, it doesn't work.

These are, I realize, very practical things, but you are plagued by practical things 365 days a year, when you are dealing with this business.

Let us pass now to software. Software meaning programs, programs of a variety of types. In other words, here you are, you have a computer centre and you are invited with open arms and the director of the computer centre says: 'Sure, you can come and use everything we have.' You say: 'Well, how about a programmer?' 'Programmer? Oh, you'll have to find your own.' 'What about programs?' 'Oh, well, I guess you have to write your own.' 'Well, how do I do that?' 'Well, you hire a programmer.' 'Hire a programmer, where?' How can you compete with large companies? I won't cite any large commercial companies, but they pay up to $20,000 a year in fees for a pro-grammer. The least little programming duty that you may have or you may wish to give out is $20 an hour with no assurance as to how many hours it will take. We tried a commercial firm once. And I still remember the result. I got nothing, and we paid an awful lot of money. That was the total result of it!

Next you have to decide what kind of languages you are going to use. This almost becomes being a prophet. You have to prophesy what programs are going to be in use for at least three or four years for the thing to be worth using. In other words, should I use Fortran? Ah, but if I use Fortran and within three years that language is no longer the one currently used, who will take care of it? No one. So I won't use that one. Cobol, or Processor, or whatever the name may be, you have to choose the program language and you have to choose the programmer according to the hardware that you have. And then you have to find a programmer who knows about the pro-gram language well enough, because just being a programmer doesn't mean that he knows that one program language in particular. You have to have a specialist for that. And more than anything he must understand what your problems are, because he's usually a commercial or scientific programmer. He has nothing to do with language. He is not used to the manipulations of words. He is concerned with the manipulation of numbers, quantities – that's it! So you have to establish that communication. Then the next step is, once you have established communication, he works for you for one year, then he has a lovely offer somewhere else and you cannot beat it. You can't com-pete. So goodbye – he goes. You get another one, it takes one year for him to learn what the other one has done and then you start all over again. These are things to keep in mind before one enters into this realm of frustration.

Finally, you have personnel problems. Not personnel problems with the people that you deal with directly, but with those who are running the equipment at the computer centre. It has happened to me so many times now that it is an old story. I go there; I bring my cards. I put them in with the program that my programmer has prepared, and I think 'Well, tomorrow I'm going to get this lovely output; now finally I'm going to see something for all this time I've spent at this.' The person operating the computer centre or the commercial company to which you go takes the cards and puts them into the card reader which is a machine which reads the cards, puts them on tape, so that the tape will go to the 7094; it will be processed, and the next stage will come and so forth. All right, so he takes the cards, and he drops them. The next day you come and there are your cards in every what order. It takes you a week to put them back together. This is poor personnel. In centres of an institutional nature the salaries are rather low, as compared to industry. As a result, people take a job at the university, at any university centre, for training purposes. They work there for a year or six months and, at the end of that time, they are trained, they know how the things work, and industry will just swipe them away for double the salary the university pays. As a result, you never get personnel that stays and is dependable. Some are, but often it isn't the case. The case of dropping the cards is, of course, an extreme, but it happens.

This is only one of the things. Then you need, of course, operators on the 7094 and the large machines, because what you have to do before a program will run is to mount different tapes; in other words, here you have a tape which contains your dictionary and here is the list of your words and you want to add that which is on your dictionary on to that which is on your list of words, and you want to put that on a new tape. Well, if it so happens that that day somebody has forgotten the ring and the process goes on, your dictionary which has taken you, let's say, a year or two to generate, is erased because somebody forgot just one little thing, the little ring which stops the fact that you can erase that tape. And there was a machine error, somebody made an error. They're human! As a result you lose your tapes. If you haven't got the cards behind you in order to regenerate your tape, you are lost. So you need good machine operators. Again, financial problems. Then you need keypunching operators; in other words, you have thought of the way in which you are going to prepare your information, everything has been well thought of, and you need somebody to keypunch. Well, you hire someone, a young lady. She learns fairly fast how to keypunch, but then she doesn't have the same interest, or the same desire, as you have for correction and exactitude. As a result, before you put your cards on to tape, you'd better print them and check to make sure there are no errors, and then if there are errors of course, you have to get cards punched again and put in the right place, but make sure they are put in the right place, and this is another problem. So again you are depending on the key-punching operator, who may be excellent so you have absolutely nothing to correct, but at any rate you'd want to check because you'd always have the doubt if you didn't. I assure you if you don't do that, by the time you come to the end of your index and you start checking your index, every three words you'll find that there is an error; the following time you'll check before it goes in.

It's quite important. This aspect, if you want, is the negative or positive aspect. In a way, I think there is something positive in anything that is negative, inasmuch that, if you know that there is a hole, you have at least a chance not to step in it. In many instances one is lured into undertakings, because one doesn't realize how deep the hole is and one steps right in it. And it's hard to get out of it once you're in it.

Next, there are basic types of programs which are required and this is what we, or rather Professor Glickman and Mr Staalman, who was the programmer for him, concentrated on, some three or four years ago. They started this series and in a way they were trying to solve four or five years ago some of the problems which are being solved elsewhere today. The first thing of course is the production of text tapes and the printing thereof. That is to say, if you are going to make a concordance of any text, you must first of all put that text on to cards, because the very internal nature of your program will dictate to you the lengths of the line you can have, the fact that you may not have hyphenated words, and a variety of context problems that you will have to solve before you can manipulate these tapes with respect to having indices, concordances, or other sorts of results. The production of a text tape and printing program that was written here cares for upper and lower case, of course, length of page, numbering of page, line numbering, diacritical marks, in the case of French and Romance languages – this is a problem that English doesn't have to the same extent. Old English, I believe, has the question of stress sometimes which you want to mark, but in French one has diacritical marks. These programs, Prora I, II, III, take care of these aspects, and give a printed output in which some of you might be interested later on. I can show you an output of this sort. That is to say, upper and lower case with diacritical marking, in the form of either prose or poetry.

The next step is programs for the production of vertical lists. Of course, once you get your text, you have to correct it. If it isn't correct, you have to repunch the cards which are wrong, you have to put your cards to tape again and print it again. This takes maybe one or two runs, if you are very lucky! But I think we all have had the problem of editing and printing a text of some sort. You know how many mistakes creep in no matter how many times you read the same passage. With my *Candide*, I read it about twenty times and I thought it was perfect and I showed it to someone and he said 'What about that?' There was one mistake left and he sure enough put his finger right on it. So there I was, I had to go through it again. But anyway, these little errors you can correct, but when they are large ones, it doesn't work that well.

Then you need a vertical list for correction. The vertical list will give you cards, if you want them, on which you will add information. Then you need at least a program for the production of a dictionary; for a reference file. For let's say that you've gone through the work of preparing a text for indexing and concordance and you've put in for each word of your dictionary, a lemma and a basic grammatical annotation. Then you want to be able to use this with another text, the next text you will be processing, since you will already have the basic information you'll be able to add it to the new text. It saves a lot of time; it saves about fifty to sixty per cent of your time for the second text. So you need some sort of a reference file, a dictionary program, which works in conjunction of course with your text file. Then you need a program for the production of indices. Indices are quite important because, if you get an index, then you can get a frequency index and you can put words in any sort of alphabetical order. Once you have a frequency index, you print all of the forms of your frequency index and then at that point you start adding lemmas, you start adding all the probabilities for these forms which you will add to all the others and this saves you fifty, sixty, or seventy per cent of the work as compared to going at it word by word. So this is absolutely necessary.

Next you need an input and output format program; in other words, how do you want this material to come out on a sheet? Do you want it to be one column, two columns, seven lines, twenty lines, starting on the sixth line from the page and so forth. Of course, what I am thinking about is a finished product which you are ready to photo-copy. This is a program that you must have. Then of course you need a general concordance program. But then you enter into all sorts of problems. What is a concordance? Is a concordance five words of the context, ten words of the context, a whole sentence? I did that for *Candide,* and this is a very difficult thing to solve because to use a full sentence context, when you have a writer who has a sentence which is a page long, means that you are going to have as many pages for just that one context as there are words in that page. Now do you realize the size of the printouts that you get for this? It's just enormous. Just for the concordance of a 35,000-word text, and I only concorded nouns, adjectives, adverbs, pronouns – no, not even pronouns, just nouns, adjectives, adverbs, and nouns, proper nouns and common nouns – I had over 1,500 pages.

Then the problem is, who is the publisher who is going to take this? It's fine to do something which is of interest, which is worthwhile, which does interest you, but then you have the problems which are going to occur after that. I'm just presenting these to you so you may have maybe a better idea of what you have to plan for. So that's why a general concordance program must be flexible. It means, you must be able to determine the context and of course that implies that when you are preparing your text you are going to have to say 'This punctuation mark is final, but this one is not.' These are types of decisions you are going to have to take for the whole text that you are dealing with. It takes quite a bit of time.

Then, you may want to go into things which I think are also interesting, inasmuch as they are the synthesis of the work on the quantitative level, that is to say, charting and plotting problems. Once you've done all this work, you can say: 'All right, I want to have a chart telling me how many proper nouns there are in such and such position or in conjunction with such and such,' and it will give you a chart of this, so that you have a pretty good idea as to what the stylistic differences are, or the context differences in this text versus another one. At first glance you can say there is a tremendous proportion of proper nouns in this text which is absolutely unusual. What is it due to? This is the case that I had with *Candide.* I've got 5,000 proper nouns in that text and there are only 35,000 words. Is this a high proportion of proper nouns; how can I explain it? Or is it perfectly logical? Does it follow suit for any of the works of Voltaire? I have no idea. This is something I have to find out later. But anyway, I can, because of these charts, at first sight say 'This text has nothing to do with this one.' There is a basic difference in the use of adjectives, of pronouns, of syntax, and so forth and so on. So you should really have those sorts of programs which are charting and plotting programs. We haven't got that here. We only got up to a concordance program which works as it can, mainly not.

Finally, what is interesting is that since you have encoded each one of these words from a syntactic viewpoint, and I would say also, if you are interested, from a semantic standpoint, what you are interested in is retrieving this information, and this is under the form of graphs. Well, that means you need syntax-analyzing programs. Now in order to set those up, this is a rather difficult job. We're trying to do something about it. But I don't know how far we'll get in the year to come. It all depends on the facilities and the ease with which we can have access to equipment on this campus.

What I can conclude from what I have presented to you is that actually what you need, what we need in the humanities, is a centre which is oriented towards the humanities rather than towards the sciences. What does that mean? The only way humanists can use computers is because there are large numbers of users in the sciences who warrant the acquisition of this equipment and the setting up of these facilities. All right, without them we cannot operate. On the other hand, one group such as, let us say, people interested in Old English, or in English in general, cannot possibly make use of that sort of equipment for a sufficient number of hours for it to be rentable. As a consequence, what you need is a centre for the humanities, wherever it would be possible, where anyone interested could go. Let us say, go for one year with a given project. There would be programmers there who know what is available, a place where all the programs that exist, the hardware which has been placed there is humanistically, if one can say so, oriented, rather than scientifically. Not that I have anything against science. I think that it's a discipline, a realm of interest like any other. But I think there is nothing really, there are no computers, oriented toward our needs, and actually we are working by charity almost, by begging for a little time, by begging for someone to help us, by begging for someone to show us how it works. As far as the usage of concordances and indices and quantitative data, or information, that can be gathered, imagination is the only boundary as to the interpretation of the results. The interest can be internal, inasmuch as you have made a concordance and indices of a given text, you can examine it, as a function of what is salient about this work: is it the syntax, is it the vocabulary? What is it? Why is it that really everyone has always taken to such a text? Is it strictly an impression? Is it an author who deals by quantity or is it by syntax and by strict antithesis? What are these characteristics? You can regroup them more rapidly if you have the tools. For instance, in the case of *Candide,* when you read the text rapidly and this happens for this sort of text, you say 'Well, there's an awful lot of crying going on in this text, you know.' There's always somebody crying. That would be the impression one would get from *Candide.* Well, if you look at the vocabulary, there is no proof at all of that. The words 'to cry' and 'tears' and so forth are a very, very small portion, almost not significant. So you have to look somewhere else. Is it in the surrounding vocabulary, or is it simply by impli-cation? Is it a text which is implicit rather than explicit? There are a variety of ways by which one can stylistically exploit this sort of work. Also, linguistically, what is interesting is to see structures which have not changed at all over a period of time. It would be quite interesting to have concor-dances going from, let us say, the eleventh to the twentieth centuries and to see whether certain syntactical structures have disappeared. What of the vocabulary has always remained, what has disappeared entirely? There are a quantity of questions one can put and I am sure that you have more to present in that respect than I have, because I am just beginning in this game. I feel that there is a reasonable use for that sort of work and that there is no reason why one should not try to exploit computers provided one knows what one is getting into.

Thank you.

ROOSEN-RUNGE I would like to respond to some of the comments of Professor Ducretet. I'm very much in agreement with his basic thrusts and I'd like perhaps to add a few arguments which I think point in the same direction, namely to some kind of centre or central pool.

I'd like to remark parenthetically that it *is* possible to obtain good programs; at least it's a little easier than Professor Ducretet indicated. But I think it takes somewhat of a shift of attitude, perhaps, on the part of the scholar. The first point is that it is very clear that one should always pay one's pro-grammers as much as one can. It is economically better to do so. Ten poor programmers will cause a lot of grief and get you nothing and one good programmer may just get you something constructive and useful. This is one place where it's not worth trying to save on salaries, as far as I've found in my experience. Also, one can get better results from programmers if one treats them more or less as professional equals, and if one can't reward them with commercial salaries, well, the scholar himself is not rewarded with salaries that he might be able to obtain outside the university, but he is being rewarded in other ways. He has a certain status as a scholar, or he would like to achieve that status. I think it's important to get the programmers interested in the work and have them get their rewards from good scholarly work in exactly the same way as their employer does. I think that if you can find ways of doing this and find ways of training people, for instance, undergraduates, to be interested in both computers and the humanities you'll find it easier to find people who can participate with you in your research in this way.

Secondly, I think that people using computers in the humanities definitely need to be more organized about how they go about it, more centralized, avoiding duplications. Some of the proposals that I've seen for work in this area have one glaring defect; that is, the proposal never says what responsibilities the scholar is going to undertake, what care he's going to take to make sure that his work is portable, that his work really can be used by people at other institutions. This means making very critical choices about programming languages, for instance, and hardware. It's not just for your own sake, to maintain the continuity of your own work, that you want to get a programming language of some life span, or to use it on a machine that's not going to disappear off the market. You want other people to make use of this work, and I frankly feel that for a lot of these projects involving large amounts of data you really cannot justify the expense, the high initial cost of putting this material into machine-readable form, if you cannot demonstrate that other scholars will be able to use that data. This initial commitment is really, I think, the important thing, and is also where it is hard to get money. I could see, if all this material, all these indices and concordances already existed, it would not be an insuperable problem for an individual scholar to look for one particular kind of thing, using perhaps an hour or two of computer time. But it's getting off the ground that's hard. That's why I think that, at this getting-off-the-ground stage, you should spend a lot of time making sure that what you do will be useful elsewhere. Of course, if you had centralized facilities, or a centre devoted to humanities, it would help.

Again, along the same lines, a scholar should take seriously what he is doing, in the sense that he should be willing to learn the techniques that are involved and not try to shove everything off on to the programmer: 'That's your field, I don't want to know anything about that, I just want to concentrate on stylistic theory or whatever.' He has to be willing to engage himself with research at all levels and recognize, I think, that at this stage of the game that we're facing today, the scholar is undertaking a kind of service responsibility. He should feel responsibility to maintain his work, maintain his programs, document them, and so on. If he isn't in a position to do that or doesn't feel that that's really part of the sort of work he'd like to do, then perhaps he simply shouldn't undertake really large projects of this sort.

DUCRETET I share Mr Roosen-Runge's viewpoint to a great extent. Not entirely though, because the problem is not granting equality of status to a fellow programmer. I have absolutely nothing against that; I don't feel superior to anyone. I think that the problem is that, in order to interest people in the humanities in the study of programming, it is very difficult to find people, first of all, who are interested, and second, who have the capacities for it. I think that the reason there is such a demand for programmers on the market today is due to the fact that there aren't enough, not even commercially. So I think we have a very small chance to attract people in the humanities unless we compete with industry, and that's rather difficult.

BAILEY I'd like to make two points: one, a response to the suggestion that we have a centre for humanistic computing. I endorse that proposal and would just like to mention one experience, concerning a scholar I won't name, but a person who spent a good deal of money getting a large body of English text on to tape. We asked if we could make use of this tape in some work that was quite unrelated to what he was up to, and offered him all the guarantees we could that it would be limited to this work that he would never conceivably be interested in. But he felt that this was not a sufficient guarantee. Well, I thought that was an unfortunate decision, but on the other hand he had spent a great deal of time and money so his reluctance was perhaps a little understandable. This is one problem, I think – if we are going to go into co-operation in a big way – that we'll have to consider the possibility of such encounters.

The other point concerns Professor Bessinger's remarks which were so optimistic. It's hard to return to that heady vision after Professor Ducretet's presentation, but while we're talking at this early point in the Conference, I'd like us to think a little – and I'd be glad to hear people speak to this – about the impact that the use of this machine will have on our discipline. There's just no question in my mind that this impact will occur. Of course, we may find ourselves thrown out on the street some morning – excluded from the discipline – but if people do enter as enthusiastically into the many aspects of computing that Professor Bessinger has mentioned, it really will reach a point where our activities are shaped by the machine. Now I don't think that's a bad thing, though I'm sure that there'll always be somebody to tell me that it is, and that will be an interesting dialogue. But this instrument, like other scientific instruments, will come to control our understanding of stylistic matters, will perhaps alter lexicography and a variety of other problems that we face. Perhaps some people who are more visionary than I might suggest what some of those might be.

SMITH I, too, speak from the machine room rather than from the library or the class-room. I want to echo or applaud practically everything you said,

Professor Ducretet, particularly the negative aspects. I think it's usually from the computer manufacturers that we get a very optimistic and hopeful commentary on what we might do, or how fast the machine is going to do our work, without any idea of how we might communicate with the machine. I think, concerning the status of the programmer, your comments were very well taken, Professor Roosen-Runge, and I think maybe the point is this. It's very rare for the programmer in a scholarly collaboration to get anything like equal billing in the final product with the scholar himself, and I think maybe this is the kind of thing you are referring to – very rare indeed, and I think this is something which should be thought about – it's not a matter of what the scholar himself thinks of his collaborator; I think it's how the collaborator ultimately appears to the world that's at issue.

Commenting on portability, I'm as great a sinner as anyone. We've said in print that the *Beowulf* concordance was produced on a 1401, a 7044, and a 7090, and that the 7044 used a Mark 2 simulator – never mind what it means – it just means that you'll never get this combination of machines in one spot again in the world. Even if we were to hand you the messy programs we produced, you couldn't possibly use them. It would be difficult anyway to hand over these programs. They're not documented. I don't want to take the time to write them up and explain to you how to use them. I don't know how to use them myself any more. I have had occasion to correspond with the producers of another volume in this series, who used completely different programs and a completely different set of machines. I asked for a copy of their program because I wanted to use their concordance generator on a machine like theirs. And they wrote a very gracious letter saying they were awfully sorry, but their program was so specific to input format that they were quite sure I would never be able to use it, and besides it wasn't documented either. So our programming work is down the drain; their programming work is down the drain; I don't know what of the programming which has gone into the Cornell series can be salvaged today. I doubt that there's a thing. I think I learned a lot; of course, that's valuable, but to me only.

BESSINGER   I say it's a good thing it's down the drain. It gives us a chance to start again and do better in a completely fresh way.

SMITH   Professor Ducretet has, I think, more faith in cards and less faith in tape than I do. I find it's frequent that cards get put out of order. I can do it myself; I don't need any computer operator to do it! I've got a version of *Paradise Lost* that is a knock-out. The rearrangement of lines produces something completely unheard of. The only solution I know is to get away from cards as soon as possible.

A final comment is just a wry one – I don't know how many times *Beowulf* has been proof-read, but are you willing to guarantee that there are no mistakes in the original text?

BESSINGER   I am not.

SMITH   Nor am I. Nor am I. We had Professor Leyerle's help proof-reading it – I believe backwards – character by character. That found a large number of mistakes after we thought it was perfect. And since then I think mistakes have cropped up. It's extremely difficult to get these things in anything like perfect condition. I don't know how Krapp and Dobbie[6] did it. I'll never understand it. You say, I think, Jess, that no typographical errors have come to light in the years since their volumes were produced.

BESSINGER   Professor Dobbie has told me with quiet, but I think pardonable, pride, that there had been no discovered errors to date in the reporting of the manuscripts. There were, of course, decisions about registering the readings of the manuscripts that he would now change, but I was very moved to hear him say this. And so far as I know that's a true statement. Professor Pope, can you tell us if that's so, to the best of your knowledge?

POPE   I thought I'd discovered a mistake the other day. I've forgotten what it is.

BESSINGER   Is that so? This is the millenium, then. I hope you'll communicate with us, sir, before the last tapes go into processing for the Krapp-Dobbie concordance.

ROBERSON   I also am with a computer centre, at the State University of New York at Binghamton. I endorse what was said about cards and tapes. I think that it's a little absurd to think of a room this size to house cards. I don't think it's essential that that be true, as long as you have enough foresight in your planning to make provision that, at some point in the steps you go through, you're sure your tape is actually representative of what you'd like to have.

I would hate to have people in this room get the impression that your experience is necessarily reflective of what everyone else would anticipate in terms of developing a concordance or a dictionary. I cannot imagine, for example in our centre, dropping cards and not being able, if there were a thousand cards, to get them back into sequence within five minutes. We do this through controls and I would stress that in any computer system mandatory controls must be imposed on both the scholar and the computer centre people to assure that the types of things you have just mentioned don't happen. I would point out, too, in terms of a couple of other specifics, that you can do a run on a 360, of course, without tying up the entire 360 through techniques that are available and something called multi-programming. You can also run programs that existed on a 1401 on a 360 through something called emulation, if you like to spend the $200 a month that it costs to do that, as opposed to paying a programmer at that point in time the cost of reprogramming.

DUCRETET   I am sure that not all centres are the same and that the facilities they have may be better in one centre than in another. I don't think that I said that one should not enter into that sort of work, I was just trying to point out

6   G. P. Krapp and E. V. K. Dobbie, *The Anglo-Saxon Poetic Records,* 6 vols. (New York, 1931-53).

SMITH   some of the experiences that concern, of course, one centre. Probably people at the centre in New York have a different experience from the one that we have here.

SMITH   A different set of problems.

DUCRETET   Yes. And I think that it varies, of course. I'm not being absolute in any way. I'm just saying that the undertaking of an Old English dictionary which I think is the reason for this conference, or one of them anyway, is a very large enterprise and that, with respect to the problems that there are in a small enterprise (I was only dealing with 35,000 items, and I may have been very unlucky, and I'm not saying I was always unlucky – I was sometimes), it should be considered beforehand, to ensure that one has the proper hardware, the proper programming facilities in the form of programmers, and that one is prepared to take on the problems that would arise and that will arise; if not those, then others. But I'm not discouraging anyone; on the contrary, as I say, negative experience is, of course, positive in many ways.

ROBERSON   May I contrast that experience with something we are doing on our campus now. We're close to finishing what will be in part a concordance of the letters of *Petrarch,* as well as a dictionary for Latin-English conversion as a result of Petrarch work. The cost, including programming time, data preparation time, as well as computer time to run this, will amount to about $12,000 to $13,000. I would like to get that in perspective. This is a work of 400,000 words.

DUCRETET   How large is your campus?

ROBERSON   We have 5,000 students.

DUCRETET   How large is your computer centre?

ROBERSON   We have 33 employees and it's a 360-40 installation.

DUCRETET   Well, that is part of the answer because you have a very small campus. Over here we have the 7094 and two 360s. There are approximately, I would say, 12,000 to 15,000 students in the sciences.

ROBERSON   I'm not sure that that has anything to do with the cost.

DUCRETET   Well, not only with the cost, it's also the access and the problems you have to having access to the computer.

ROBERSON   I think that's a problem anywhere.

DUCRETET   And this is also a time problem because, if you have a programmer, you can't say 'Well, look we can only work when we have access to the computer.' You have to pay him all year round. He has to live also. So there are a variety of problems that may have arisen which are unique to this campus and which may have been caused by my own fault.

HATCH   I just wanted to make a very brief suggestion. That is, if the documentation of the program is as important as it seems to be from what I've heard, it might be that the programmer should be responsible for making his documentation and that it be put in as part of whatever the final result of the work is. That is, with a concordance that the documentation be part of what is presented. This would allow also for the programmer to get whatever credit is due to him for the amount of work that he did on this particular project.

BESSINGER   This of course raises immediate questions of copyright and patent which I understand is a topic undergoing a good deal of scrutiny in different places today, though hardly ever by lawyers. Programmers are very concerned about it, but there have been no legal decisions and no precedents as yet established on this very important matter, and the United States Bureau, the Copyright Bureau, the Patent Bureau, are not interested at all in encouraging software applications for patents, as indeed, would seem to be practical today.

HATCH   If they were printed, it seems to me it would somewhat change the category of the copyright.

BESSINGER   Yes. Those laws are very complicated, as you know, and we are all of us going to face this problem very soon about what programs we use, and of protecting them, and of amalgamating them. It is not a subject I can speak on with any authority at all, but I am simply appalled at the legal tangle that apparently we are going to face fairly soon in this regard.

MITCHELL   I should like to ask a question really revealing my ignorance once again. The question is this. We have heard a little about the obsolescence in computers and I understand this is a practical problem. In the case of the corpus of *The Anglo-Saxon Poetic Records* we already have available everything in the form in which it can be put on to a machine in a machine-readable form. We have the text there, agreed and useful. So what is the position about Old English prose? At the moment we have some excellent editions, and we have some that are clearly archaic which will have to be redone; we have some things which have never been printed; they still exist only in manuscripts. The question I would like to ask is this. If the machines are going to become obsolete in time, are we really compelled to wait until we have all the Old English prose texts properly edited before we can do anything about putting anything on to the tape? I mean, this is a practical proposition as to how long any machine is going to exist which will be valuable to us and how compatible the programs are if we start now and maybe have to wait twenty years.

SHOOK   Mr Bessinger?

BESSINGER   No, I was going to yield the floor to Dr Smith on this for a moment.

SMITH   I, myself, am not half so concerned with the obsolescence of machines as of now, beginning now. If we program in so-called higher languages, like Fortran, conceivably PL 1, the languages we can be sure are going to be around, I myself will be very surprised if the next generation of machines will not accept Fortran programming and probably Cobol, Algol, and PL 1 programming. I think this business of obsolescence is going to be like last year's car being obsolete because this year's car is better. But last year's car still runs. This was not true, perfectly true, in the case of the 7094. The programs written in machine language for the 7094 just don't work on a new machine, but people, I think, decreasingly write programs which are specific to one machine and they increasingly write programs in the so-called higher languages which will run on a wide variety of machines. I don't think that's a problem.

MITCHELL   It was just a question.

SMITH   I don't know whether you agree?

ROOSEN-RUNGE   Well, I think you're in a paradox here, because, again, you have conflicting scholarly demands. It seems to me you have one kind of demand for an initial large amount of output in a variety of forms; items sorted in many different ways, categorized in different ways. Then you have the subsequent use of the same data base for which new programs have to be written. Now, it seems to me that the preparation of the first large flow of output is going to be very expensive if you write in higher-level languages. You can usually save some time, and therefore money, if you can get a programmer to write machine language. If you start out on small machines, which may happen at a small campus for instance, then the higher-level languages are even more inefficient and it's much more natural to go to machine language. I have the feeling that what you want to try to do is get the best of both worlds. You want to try, perhaps, to do large projects once very efficiently, then make the data base available in a form which is compatible with almost any high-level language going around, so that the individual scholar who only wants to use it once, to get one kind of thing out, can write his own program in high-level language. The trouble is, if you write in machine language it costs you programming time and saves you execution time.

SHOOK   Is there any other reply to Dr Mitchell's question?

DUCRETET   I would like to answer perhaps in a different way. I would think that if a centre were established, certain equipment would be there for a period of time; I mean to say, that you would know it would be there for the next ten years. This equipment would be available and would be maintained and under those conditions you could start doing something long range. Whereas, what is happening is that, in most cases today, the places where the computers are, are either commercial or university systems or centres and, of course, what they want to do is to keep up-to-date. I think perhaps that one of the solutions would be to choose the best way at a given time and not to dispose of it until the date that one has set has come and everything that one prepared is finished. Now that wouldn't mean that one would not foresee the use of something else at another stage, but it would give a certain stability, and I think the problem for humanists is that there is such a rapid change occurring that one cannot really undertake a work of five or ten years because the chances are that by the end of three or four years something else will have occurred which will, if not invalidate, at least threaten considerably the work which one has already done. Perhaps that might be a solution for a centre for the humanities, or for Old English.

MITCHELL   Thank you very much.

CUMMINGS   I'd like to add something to your remarks. I think that some of the problems we have been discussing will be solved in part by the concept of some sort of centre or consortium. Because not only will an Old English project be attracted to such a centre but perhaps other humanistically oriented projects might well be. The result is that there is a demand. The computing centre director is interested in getting equipment. If the demand is sufficient, I think that – to change Professor Bailey's idea a bit – rather than the equipment directing our research, we will direct the design of equipment to suit our needs if we have a sufficient demand. As for the people who are so valuable to the development of the scholar's programs, I think these people will gradually be trained at any place that has a very large computer centre, because presumably it is training these people already in the various kinds of scientific, mathematical, and practical engineering orientations. Some of these people might well be humanistically trained, so long as there is some kind of a market for whatever it is that they learn by working with scholars.

DUCRETET   May I answer that? I think that although we are numerous here, with respect to the use of any centre, the voice that we would have wouldn't be very loud. For instance, I think that the terminal for engineering here at the University of Toronto has a turnover of about 2,000 jobs a day, and I don't think the humanities could possibly use the computers more than a few hours every month or so, because the preparation is so great. So I don't foresee the solution that you are precognizing for the simple reason that I don't think there is enough demand for any computer to be built which would solve the problems we have, and which would be rentable. I don't think that this is feasible in the near future.

BESSINGER   I hope you're wrong because we are trying to build such a centre right now.

DUCRETET   I wasn't thinking of the centre, I was thinking of the hardware.

BESSINGER   The hardware has to be the hardware that's there already, in several large university centres and must be made available to Old English specialists, and I think will be. We have some assurance that this will happen. Dr Smith?

SMITH   I don't know whether it is hopeful or not. IBM has a small group of people on some high management level whose responsibility is to go around among humanists and ask them what their needs are in computers – and one of them came to us at New York University last year. We wrote down some of our hardware ideas and software ideas, but my own bias is that, given a computer with its strengths and limitations, I naturally try to do my work within these constraints. I guess I sort of agree with you, Professor Ducretet. I am gloomy about IBM spending a million dollars to introduce a hardware instruction that would help me or you, or any of us. I think that IBM might very well say to us, 'Well, you know you could do that with three steps now, and we're not going to introduce the instruction to do it in one step.' I don't know, I don't consider this a problem. The comment was made that the computer is a scientific machine – I forget how it was put – it doesn't matter. It seems to me that a computer is a computer, and I can't imagine a computer being any more humanistic than today's computers are, or tomorrow's computers will be. This is the nature of the physical beast. It's a tool, about like a screwdriver. It's completely flexible. You say a certain language is a flexible language or a certain language is an expressive language – speaking of the existing human languages. Similarly it seems to me that human language is a tool. We use it as we will, and I feel the same way about computers. They may be more or less easy to manipulate, to program. They may be more or less expensive in doing a certain job, but any computer is a computer and if we come to it with Old English it does one thing and if somebody comes to it to design a bridge it does something else. So I'm not sure that there is any such thing as a computer more humanistically oriented than it is today.

BAILEY   When I mentioned the limitations of the computer shaping some of our wishes, I didn't mean it on such a low level, though perhaps you weren't responding to that. In any case, I certainly understand that the computer is a general purpose machine, that's its virtue, right. But now I was thinking more of the kind of thing that I. A. Richards has to say in *Speculative Instruments* (Chicago, 1955) in which he tries to point out that the device that you use to aid your seeing controls your seeing, as simple as that. Now, as abstract as that, I might add too. And we're far from being troubled by this, I suppose, we have many more ideas than we can execute even now. But, well eventually we are going to come up against this problem, in an interesting philosophical way. I don't know who's thinking about this. I hope somebody.

HAMMER   I wonder about the obsolescence question asked in reverse. In other words, is it possible to anticipate technical developments? Is there some level of predictability in the way computers are being developed now so that a large-scale project, where preparatory work will take a number of years, can be conceived of in such a way that it will mesh, or so that you are anticipating the kind of computer that's going to be available say, five or ten years from now – or twenty years? I just wondered if there was a level of predictability in computer development.

ROBERSON   I'm not sure computer manufacturers know what's going to be twenty years from now. A number of people here were at Penn. State a few months ago where we addressed something similar to this, and we tried to encourage people there to think in terms of flexibility in the design of whatever they are attempting to do. In other words, if you constrain yourself to fixed limitations based on a specific project, then the chances are you may well be obsolete with any innovation in computing or software. However, if you can broaden your parameters, even though you may not need them at that time, and build in the necessary flexibility that might allow more than just yourself to use a particular set of programs for something like *Beowulf,* then the likelihood of your becoming obsolete in the near future is more remote. I hope that's an answer, but I think it's as definite as we can be in the circumstances.

ROOSEN-RUNGE   I think there are some technological developments which are hopeful for the humanities. It might be worth reiterating the point which Professor Ducretet made, that computers were originally designed for scientific computation. That meant that the ability to take in, in one gulp, large amounts of data was not a critical factor, but the ability to do long sequences of highly repetitive operations very quickly was important. My impression is that the computing power that the humanities needs is really a kind of duplication of the scientific requirements in that the actual logical sophistication of most programs in the humanities is really very low inside, where the computer is doing what it can do best, while the sophistication of input and output control format, etc., is very great and far exceeds that which the scientist normally demands. Now the technological innovations that I think will help here are, first, optical photo-readers. They exist now and it's quite conceivable that the ability to take printed material of a variety of fonts directly into machine-readable form is going to increase with the passing years. At the moment it's too expensive to be practical unless you are going to restrict yourself to one not very aesthetic type fount or perhaps one of two or three possible founts. The second thing is that bulk storage which is very crucial with large amounts of data is becoming increasingly available and the cost of this is going down per bit. This is storage which holds a lot, but it takes a little longer to get to any piece of it. In contrast to tape storage, it's a kind of storage which you can get at every individual part of the data, if you want a single word or a single sentence, in roughly the same amount of time, whereas, of course, on a tape if the thing is on the end, it requires reading through everything on it first. So I think that these kinds of things do lie on the horizon. When you first hear about them, they are always too expensive, but the experience in the past has been that the cost of computing power and the cost of random-access storage have steadily dropped.

RIGG   Would you like to expand a bit on the photo-reading? This seems to me one of the most useful things which could come out of computers for humanistic purposes and a lot of us would really like to know what the future is.

ROOSEN-RUNGE   Well, I'm really not an expert on it. I've practically shot my wad. I know that these devices exist. I think that the Social Securities Administration in the United States has used devices made by IBM. That's all I can say. I don't think they are something you can use at the moment because you have to prepare the printed information for them in a particular fount. Perhaps other people know more about that.

SMITH   May I comment? So far as I know the Social Security machine that you speak of reads numbers typed by employers, numbers in a variety of typewriter founts, and does so rather well. But it's numbers, and they are all of a given spacing, that is, the ones are as wide as the sixes, which is not true of the *m*'s and the *i*'s in normal printed texts. I did once talk to some of the people at IBM who had worked on the Social Security machine and asked why we couldn't take *The Anglo-Saxon Poetic Records* to that machine or a similar one. And their answer was what they call the pitch problem, which is just the varying width of the letters. The business of the unattractive – that wasn't quite your word ...

ROOSEN-RUNGE That was what I intended.

SMITH ... funny-looking type is, I believe, the ability of the machines to read a certain strange type-fount with the whole alphabet plus a number of other characters typed on a specific selectric typewriter.

ROOSEN-RUNGE Philco

SMITH Oh, there may be a Philco machine too. There is a machine which will read the product of a selectric typewriter with a special golfball which you and I can read and that's all very well, but somebody still has to sit there and copy the Old English on this typewriter. It doesn't avoid the step of keyboarding, so-called. I think it would be better than the keypunch. I haven't tried it; it sounds better than the keypunch. But somebody's still got to do it. In other words, I still don't think this machine is adequate, nor do I have any idea that there ever will be one to which we can take the Krapp-Dobbie, even if we were willing to have the pages cut up – let's sacrifice a copy – and come away with a magnetic tape. I can't get anybody to tell me anything which gives me any hope that that's on the horizon. Now, does somebody else have some hope?

BELL Yes. Most of the information we get about optical readers seems to come through very corrupt oral tradition. I get diametrically opposed views from IBM people and others. But it seems to me that this is an exciting prospect if a device such as, say, Lederle's flying-spot scanner, which he uses for chromosome typology, or even some kind of pulse-code modulation, could be used to read things even like manuscripts; then we could get at more empirical paleographical criteria – even for runological typology and things like that. We could start at a much earlier process – not wait, let's say, for edited Anglo-Saxon prose texts and then input edited texts. It would serve to establish new editorial criteria on a more empirical basis this way.

BAILEY I hope that anybody who is genuinely interested in this subject will talk to Professor Venezky. At the Dictionary of American Regional English in Madison they do use the golfball that you mention and it produces a type which looks something like the numbers on your bank cheques, and then this in the normal course of things is run through a machine made by the Control Data Corporation and this is the basis for much of what they are doing on that dictionary. It doesn't avoid the key-boarding side, but it is something that can be done by a normal typist and is less expensive than keypunch.

DUCRETET On that subject, I have here *Computers and the Humanities,* a publication of Queens College, which I guess you all know about, and there is an article here, 'Optical Readers' by R. S. Morgan.[7] The notes he has at the end say 'Professor John Horty at the Health Law Center, Pittsburgh, uses an optical page reader. Professor John C. Lyons of the Computer-in-Law Institute at the George Washington University has also used page readers extensively, and Professor S. J. Skelly and I are also experimenting with the medium at the University of Manitoba.' So obviously there are some which are operational.

SMITH   Does it mean that they are taking a printed page from the library shelf to the optical reader? That's what I'm not clear on.

BESSINGER   It certainly doesn't state that.

DUCRETET   It doesn't state that, yes.

SHOOK   Is there anyone else who would like to speak before this session closes? Professor Bessinger, Professor Ducretet, on behalf of the group here, I want to thank you for your reports and for the interesting comments, questions, they have provoked, and I want to thank all who have participated from the floor. I'm looking forward to an exciting meeting in the morning.

7   R. S. Morgan, 'Optical Readers,' *Computers and the Humanities,* III (1968), 61-64.

saturday morning

COMPUTER CONCORDANCES IN PROGRESS

CAMERON Good morning. This morning is a rare occasion; we have a complete table full of people who have been working on concordances of Old English texts. What we will do this morning is begin with fairly brief reports on each of the projects underway and then Professor Venezky has some proposals to make on computer processing of Old English texts. We would like to begin with the Old English concordance to *Beowulf,* by Professor Bessinger and Dr Smith.

BESSINGER Thank you. I shall make my remarks very brief, partly because all of the technical questions that anyone is liable to ask should be raised from the floor, and asked to Dr Smith; and partly because a review of these matters is now available in the Editor's Preface and the Programmer's Preface to *A Concordance to Beowulf.* The first page of the Editor's Preface is even more poignant than I thought it was, when I wrote it about three years ago. It begins somewhat coyly with a quotation from Albert S. Cook's *A Concordance to Beowulf* (Halle, 1911):

> This concordance to *Beowulf* was prepared some years ago, as the first instalment of a projected concordance to the complete extant remains of Old English poetry. As that larger compilation has not in the meantime been made, there seems no sufficient reason for longer withholding from publication a book which ought to prove useful to those who seriously occupy themselves with this remarkable poem.

One could almost weep reading that paragraph. For what it is worth, our full concordance to the complete Krapp-Dobbie *Anglo-Saxon Poetic Records* is farther along than Cook's was in 1911. We have completed a little pilot project, the concordance to *Beowulf,* which we thought it would be fun to do and to, so to speak, measure up against Cook's, and see where his was better and where ours was better – to learn lessons that we could apply in the preparation of the complete *Poetic Records.* The complete *Poetic Records* have all been taped – we have them on disc as well; we have a raw concordance printout from it; we have had it for over two years. We are sitting now waiting for free machine time and some machinery to do the last updating of the concording tapes with. There is no reason in principle why Cornell could not go ahead and publish it next week in the new photo-composition process which will be a good deal more handsome than the selectric golfball process by which we printed the *Beowulf.* I don't wish to speak disrespectfully of the appearance of these pages because the designer of them, the artist, I should say, who designed this book, is sitting at my left and it is extremely hard to design a beautiful book on a computer. Anyone who makes a gesture in that direction, and who succeeds as well as Dr Smith did with the, I think, very handsome double-column format with automatic cross-indexing, automatic keyword frequency-listing, automatic tags at the top of columns, automatic paging, and all the rest of it, all done, you see, months and years before the actual printout was photo-reduced and published – anyone who can do that on a computer is something close to a magician. It is hard enough to design a beautiful page, or even a readable one, if you are a publishers' designer and have the proper tools and go at it in the regular bibliographical way. But to do it on a computing console seems to me a peculiar feat of wizardry.

Well, Dr Smith will tell you that we used four machines in six different stages in this process. We punched cards on a 1401; various 1401 programs were then done to update, to correct, the master tape whenever errors were found – *our* errors, which we found frequently. Automatic verification could have been done at this stage but we did not do it; we decided to proof-read by hand and by eye. I wish now that we had done the automatic verification too and then proof-read *that* by eye and by hand. The text was concorded on a 7090 IBM machine in two versions, one with and one without hyphens. These versions were inserted by the editor into an index list prepared by the programmer, and the two texts were then merged so that both the hyphenated forms and the non-hyphenated forms would show in the final headword list, but not in the text citations. We more than doubled the amount of verbal and lexical information in our book as compared with Cook's concordance. Cook omitted about 500 of the most frequently occurring 'unimportant' words. Believing that in the first place machines should be made to do all of the work and pick up every last little scrap and crumb of information, we resolved not to omit any unimportant words. Those unimportant words are for certain purposes of grammar and stylistic study as important as any other words in the language – maybe the most important. So all of our words are there, and a good many more words are in our text than are in Dobbie's text of the Cotton Vitellius codex because we hyphenated Dobbie's text and automatically cross-referenced all of those hyphenations so that the second half of compounds would not be lost. We hyphenated many words, not just adjectives and nouns, in a desperate effort to get as much information as we could from the text.

The text was concorded on the 7090 machine; then, as I said, we merged tapes, brought together the hyphenated and the non-hyphenated forms of the text. Then the 1401 merged the 7090 versions to create the automatic cross-indexing that we desired and to accept card corrections on headword lines, to make orthographic adjustments in the word listings, as the form ð and so on. Then the 7044 program edited the text into two-column pages. Then, back on the 1401, a program punched new cards from the 7044 tape output and these cards were used to drive the 1050 typewriter terminal with the selectric golfball on it which printed the final output, ready for photo-reduction and offset printing. At that stage it had upper and lower case and capitalized headwords and automatic frequency numbers and catchwords at the tops of columns and all the rest of it, neatly designed and, I think, flawlessly printed out on typographical principles. There may be a few little

things in there that we would like to correct next time around but it seems
to me to have run off remarkably quickly and well and all of this is thanks
to Dr Smith.

Now it *did* take three years. That's a very small text indeed on which to
spend three long years and we could only justify this to ourselves because
it was to be a pilot job, to be subsumed, with changes, in the complete
Anglo-Saxon Poetic Records. I shall not try to list all the things that we
learned, but one of the lessons in machine programming of literary texts is,
I think, hard not to learn. That is that it is best to let the machine do unaided
as much as you can of the big job, to interfere with it as little as possible, to
resolve that a machine concordance is different in kind from a manual concordance and that this is not necessarily a bad thing. I would urge, for
example, that a machine concordance of the *Beowulf* must be at present a
concordance of an edition, not of a manuscript. This puts the responsibility
for the edition squarely where it belongs, on the edition's editor, and the
responsibility for checking that edition squarely where it belongs, on the
concordance's user. It allows the concordance itself merely to be as accurate
a record of the edition itself, as lavish or as laconic, as one wishes it, and as
one can design it.

There are some special features of this book which I hope readers of it
will find useful. At one stage in this processing Dr Smith gave me a simply
astonishing printout of what he told me would be a KWIC concordance, a
keyword in context concordance, which could be arranged automatically
to produce a long textual citation of about five verse pairs with the concorded matter in the centre of the page. We published a long appendix in
this fashion – I don't think you can see it from where you are sitting – with
the headwords now in the centre of the page. The headwords, moreover,
are not words but groups of words which form repetitive phrases. I will not
use the word 'formulaic,' since not all exact repetitions are formulas. This
machine was told to bring together all identical strings of letters and spaces
for x number of characters. This is a twelve-character KWIC concordance.
And so it shows all of the groups in the poem which are exactly alike as to
twelve characters. One can of course instruct the machine to give an eleven-
character or fourteen-character index. We did so instruct the machine, in
fact, and were deluged with paper. Various KWIC concordances of the same
poem gave us very different impressions of the formulaic consistency of the
poem. I mentioned this fact yesterday; it's as if the machine were asking us
questions. 'What do you *mean* by a formulaic poem?' the machine will say,
'I can give you any number of formulaic poems.' They are all in Cotton
Vitellius and the machine demands that you, the scholar, the reader, decide
what kind of formulaic parameter you want to search for. It will quite wit-
lessly give you repetitions that are not formulaic at all, as I was saying. Mere
accidents of spelling will produce things like 'secgan hyrdon' or 'fyrena
hyrde' together. They are not remotely formulaic, nor are 'Ne mæg byrnan

byrnan hring' and 'byrnan hringdon.' There are just enough characters together to constitute a formulaic-looking sequence in this case, but the
formulas are phony: they are merely typographical. There are some questions that may or may not be phony that I don't know how to discuss. If
you throw away patronymic expressions like 'bearn Ecgþeowes' of which
there may be any number, then the poem's remaining formulaic expressions
tend to group themselves in pairs; occasionally in triplets, but most often in
pairs. The *Beowulf* poet, or poets, was overwhelmingly fond of two formulaic expressions, and I cannot explain this if the poem is the product of
some oral tradition or if it is the product of some very conscious lettered
tradition. Either way it seems a very strange economy, or thrift, that is being
exploited here in a strange fashion. You get these pairs, overwhelmingly. I
must ask you to look at the book to prove it; you get these pairs overwhelmingly no matter what parameters you chose, whether you wanted a twelve-
character KWIC concordance, or a ten- or fifteen-character KWIC concordance,
or whatever. The pairing is simply there, somehow, in the texture of the
diction, style, vocabulary of the poem, and I don't know how to explain it.
I hope, not today, but sometime soon, that there will be a sufficient expla-
nation.

Anyway, as you see, the process of making this little concordance has
given us food for thought. It has taught us some lessons about how to
proceed and some things not to do. We think we can do more now with the
complete Krapp-Dobbie text than we did with the *Beowulf.* For one thing,
we will have better machines, and we will have a much more lavish final
printing process, thanks to the Cornell Press. But these are details. The
concordance generator will be the same with minor changes. In large, I
think it would be fair to say that the complete Krapp-Dobbie will be pretty
much a bigger version of this small *Beowulf* concordance. The Krapp-Dobbie
raw concordance that I spoke of has been finished for several years and sits
in my office in four elephantine folio volumes. It is all one can do to lift one
of them at a time. It has been exasperating that there has been no way to
translate these completed printouts, perfectly readable pages, into publishable form; but there they are, and the resulting complete concordance, if
we make it as complete as we want to, will be huge. I suppose it will be in
two volumes, very large volumes. The alternative to that, of course, is to cut
down the number of unimportant words, or stop words, to use Professor
Venezky's useful term. One can give the stop words not with line-contexts
but simply with index numbers supplied. This would put the material at the
disposal of anyone who wanted it but would not clutter the pages of the
final, rather expensive, concordance with twenty-five pages of 'ands.' However, some of these matters of design, of book design and editorial design,
remain still to be settled. I think I will stop short now so that you can ask
Dr Smith any technical questions and perhaps raise special questions about
the book that I have not covered. Mainly, though, I hope you will come up

and look at the book. I had hoped to be able to send a train-load of them up here for this meeting, to present everyone with a copy as a sort of favour for the party, but this proved impossible. So far, I have only had my hands on this one copy. It's beginning to show it, but I hope you will all come up to look at it and ask questions about it.

Thank you.

ROBERSON   Sir? You did this on a selectric typewriter?

BESSINGER   The final product was from a selectric machine, yes.

ROBERSON   Would you do that again?

BESSINGER   We went through three different technologies – this is what I was saying yesterday about obsolescence. We had print wheels made; we never even got to fitting them on the machine. The machine was changed before we got to use them. We had slugs made for print chains and finally made cuff links out of the slugs. We never got to putting them on the machine, either. And then, finally, we had a cheap little selectric golfball made and, *quickly,* before anything could happen, ran off the concordance on it!

ROBERSON   Would that be your option in the future?

BESSINGER   No, no indeed, no. No.

ROBERSON   I would think that, that's why I asked.

BESSINGER   No, we wouldn't think of using again that model which we designed; it's two years old.

SMITH   It's terribly slow, as you can imagine, and it is actually subject to mechanical error which I don't think I have ever seen in a computer printer. I don't think ever in my life I've seen a real computer error, I mean a real error from inside the electronics of a computer. At one point we printed the text, not the concordance but the text, on the golfball with the 1050 for proof-reading, with the idea that in upper and lower case and þ's and ð's it might be a little easier to proof-read than the raw computer form of it. And in it there were three mistakes in 3,000 lines which I was able to convince myself by re-doing were the result of the printer, of the golfball itself, not the result of anything else – which is, for the computer world, a high error rate. But there was much more wrong with it than that – I mean, time mainly.

COLLINS   Is there any way in which you can show in this concordance words which are reconstructed, doubtful readings, or actual interpolations, words which were not in the manuscript at all?

BESSINGER   This gave us a simply hellish time. Our copy-text is Elliott Dobbie's text of *Beowulf* and I think it might be simpler if I read from a paragraph in our book. 'We listed for concording every word in Dobbie's text except the fragmentary *le* at line 240 (Klaeber's [*hwī*]*le.*' (p. xiv) But we suppressed Dobbie's square brackets – this was a shocking thing to do, a very naughty thing to do – but we suppressed them, along with his italics, which, you remember, represent the letters adopted in one of the Thorkelin transcripts, one or the other, sometimes both. Dobbie has an awful lot of information in his text about those transcripts. We could not reproduce this material.

There was no economical way. We omitted the italics because our typographical process does not have an italic fount and because we wanted to
save our underlining feature for runic expressions, which are, however,
insignificant in *Beowulf* – there is only the logogram ᛟ – but in the complete
Krapp-Dobbie we wanted to use these italics for runic information. But
more importantly, the square brackets were dropped because, while all
bracketed material in Dobbie is conjectural, not all conjectural material is
bracketed. On the first page, line 6, 'eorlas,' manuscript 'eorl'; Dobbie's
text gives no sign *in the text of the poem* that the 'as' has been added.
There is, of course, a footnote on the page to tell you this. On line 139,
'sohte,' the word appears in roman without any sign that it has been supplied by conjecture. Again no sign in the text. Line 2001, the word 'micel'
appears in brackets, in square brackets, and is obviously a very conjectural
form; Dobbie has gone out of his way to call it to your attention, but
he has got three kinds of restoration going and he only shows one square
bracket set. We thought there was nothing honest to do but suppress those
brackets. What we have given is a very mechanical guide to the study of
Dobbie's text of the poem, with no indication in the concordance about
matters of textual criticism. I regret this, and we are going to find some
way if we possibly can in the complete Krapp-Dobbie to show conjectural
forms – italics or asterisks or something, for, in a very big book, this will be
much more necessary than in the case of the concordance to *Beowulf*.
Everyone knows *Beowulf* by heart anyway, and anyone who uses this text
will be sufficiently familiar with the poem, I think, to be willing to go to
other kinds of reference works for the kind of information the textual
critic wants, the kind of information the scholar's grammar provides. This
finding list is not a grammar, it does not parse the poem, it does not interpret the text of the poem; it simply sends you to Dobbie's edition for any
further information.

 I must sound very defensive about this. We have for years been trying to
think of ways to get various rather subtle bits of textual information into
the concordance and there seems no way to do it. I think now we can perhaps think of ways to introduce some of it. Thank you for that question.
I hope it clears the air a little bit; it doesn't clear my conscience.

BELL Was the decision on the two-column format instead of, say, the KWIC index
 format, one of spatial economy?

SMITH No, I don't think that was it. We were just going to present the verse pair
 with each as the context for each citation. The KWIC that we did present,
 and it is in this volume, is really very much an afterthought. It was kind of
 a little game just to see what would come out, and it was sort of interesting.
 I'm not getting the message across to you – I don't think I've answered your
 question – but I'm not really quite sure that we thought very much about a
 KWIC presentation. I think I was sort of against a KWIC presentation at one
 time in my life for some reason I no longer believe in. Did we talk about a
 KWIC – doing the whole thing in KWIC form?

BESSINGER   Yes, we did. Professor Frederic Cassidy suggested that, and strongly urged that if possible we put the whole concordance into the KWIC format. I wanted not to do this, because it seemed to me that this would suppress one very valuable piece of instant information given by the regular verse-pair format, and that is simply rhythmical or metrical information. Whatever else this non-grammatical grouping of information does, it shows you Sievers' and Pope's scansion materials together. You see, we could have chosen to do citations at any length and with any amount of evidence, as Cook did, for example, by ellipses and abbreviation, to show a semantic and syntactic unit in each case. The verse-pair context is of course sometimes syntactic but most often not, as a unit; but it does show a *verse* pair and forces one's attention to that one very important piece of prosodic factual data. A KWIC concordance would not obliterate the verse pair but would tend to submerge it in a vast long line where it would not stand out. This is a weak justification for not using the KWIC but that was one of the things we thought about. The other was that it is hard to design the KWIC pages. Books are wrong in shape for the KWIC concordance. We had to turn the book up on end to do the appendix.

BELL   It would have been a good deal longer.

BESSINGER   Very much longer, yes. And the Press was already worried about book size. We must of course think about publishers and their economic requirements as soon as we start thinking about a book of this kind. It is going to have to go through a publishing house sooner or later, and those people are very thoughtful indeed about matters like the largest number of pages you can have in a book before the human binders cannot bind the book. You cannot go over 1,010 pages of certain quality paper because the stitches won't hold. That's it. If your concordance format happens to run 1,020 pages, it is an impossible length. Our press didn't have the facilities to give us a long, low book instead of a long, tall one. Things like this, I am afraid, influenced us more than they should have; we did lots of things for no theoretical reason, but just because the realities of publishing pressed us.

SMITH   I'd appreciate it – I have a little note here saying to remind me to ask users to let us know the shortcomings and perhaps even strengths of the book so that we have a better idea what to do with the six volumes of ASPR and if, for example, a lot of people voted for a KWIC presentation, there may be ways in which we can do it. I mean we can have just this much KWIC; that is, it is about 100 characters left to right which is not a whole lot less than this KWIC line. I chose 120 characters here because that is what you get on a computer printer and in the first presentation of this that is a convenient number of characters to use, but we needn't be limited by that. We can have 150 characters if you have enough paper, or we can have 90 characters, if that's all we have.

BESSINGER   You'd go into three or four volumes if you did that, because you couldn't have double columns.

SMITH   Right! But in the six-volume ASPR we will have a lot more foldbacks, we think – if you will pardon me, lines, verse pairs, which take two lines to print – I think we should have a lot more of them because we are going to have a lot more identification – we have only the line number in the *Beowulf* and that was enough to identify the source, but we have got to say it is *Beowulf* when we do the six volumes, or we've got to say it's psalm such and such, or whatever poem it is. So we may have more foldbacks anyway. And if a large number of people felt that a KWIC presentation was really more useful, it might pay to do it like that. I don't know what it cost, but it was very considerable.

BESSINGER   The cost would be frightful. But here is the answer to the double-column format problem, for example. Cook's concordance contained 436 pages and has just under half as much lexical information in it as ours does which is exactly half the size, because of the double-column format. Even after the multiplying of entities by editorial surgery on the hyphenation system.

WHALLON   My neighbours and I don't know what KWIC means.

BESSINGER   KWIC – it sounds like a breakfast food! It's K.W. I. C. – it means 'Key word in context' and it is a sort of traditional word I suppose applied to the process by its inventor, and this acronym has stuck.

SMITH   It contrasts with KWAC which is 'key word out of context,' which is what we call an index, isn't it?

REIDY   You say the final printout was done on a golfball – was this golfball made with þ's and ð's?

SMITH   That's the thing, exactly. It had to do with money. For about $1,200 we could have had slugs made for the printer to our specification.

BESSINGER   We did have them made. The most expensive cuff links I've ever owned.

SMITH   Exactly. Those were off the shelf though. Those were Icelandic characters – at least, I guess that's where they come from.

BELL   Yes! IBM Iceland does have a type fount with þ's and ð's. I think it's only upper case.

SMITH   Exactly! We got these ugly upper-case characters with the idea that we would at least have that, and when we finally got the slugs on the chain experimentally they were 5,000ths of an inch or some small, but visible, distance above or below the rest of the print line, in addition to being unattractive, at least the form was unattractive. But we didn't have lower case anyway, and to have these made would have cost $200 a character and there are six characters, þ, ð, and æ upper and lower case. Then we found that you could get a golfball made (not by IBM, by another company) which was going to cost a tenth or a hundredth as much as IBM's, and for about $250 we got these characters put on a golfball. In fact, what they do is they have a golfball on their shelf and I imagine they grind off the character that you don't want and glue on the character you do want and quite literally you can see on the golfball that something like this has been done.

BESSINGER   You won't believe it, but the glue has not yet become unstuck on this model T golfball.

REIDY   IBM once gave a demonstration of this which would be very useful for speeding up the Middle English dictionary. Then I asked them what it would cost to produce a golfball with six extra characters on it. They didn't really know but they mentioned an enormous figure and I said 'Well, that's impossible.'

SMITH   They are impossible.

BESSINGER   We can give you names and agents.

SMITH   I just happen to have the address of the company here. The first golfball cost, I think, $250, and the second golfball cost $111, that is, we had to pay for the creation of the so-called 'art-work' to create the lower-case printout. No, the digraph was available in a sans-serif type style, which is why this is sans-serif, from Denmark or some place. We had to pay to have þ and ð made, the upper and lower cases. Four 'art-works' at $50 apiece. That was a one-time charge and those are there for all of you to use now. You don't have to pay that now. You can have your own golfball for $111, which I think was the cost of the second one. Well, this is still more than an off-the-shelf golfball. If you want to type Old English you can type Old English in this type style for that price, if you have a selectric typewriter. I do have the name of the company. They are just wonderful to deal with, they are just as nice as they can be.

BESSINGER   They redesigned our þ four different times for us because we didn't like it and we kept sending it back and telling them to do the ascender differently, and so on, and this was good fun. The IBM designers would not have been so tolerant.

SMITH   And when it finally came, one of the characters didn't fit quite right - it was very faint – so we sent it back and it came back and it printed a little better. You can see it's not perfect, but it's better.

CAMERON   I would like now to ask Professor Venezky of the University of Wisconsin to talk about his concordances to the Rushworth Matthew and Vercelli Homilies.

VENEZKY   Before saying a few short words about concordances I would like to express my appreciation to the Centre for Medieval Studies; to Professor Leyerle, to Professor Cameron and, of course, to Mrs Higgs, for the magnificent arrangements. For those of us reared on MLA encampments this is quite a pleasant experience.

   The concordances that we are working on at Wisconsin are to the Homilies in the Vercelli book and to the Rushworth Matthew. The Vercelli Homilies are being done principally by Professor Jon Erickson of the English Department; I am adding some very small role to the editing and translation and a rather large role to the computer processing. The Rushworth Matthew is my own, and I will somehow have to defend what I am doing there at some later date. Professor Erickson worked with the original manuscript of the Vercelli book; Ruthworth is being done to the Skeat edition of the Holy Gospels. We're retaining superscripts, expansions, restorations, and one size of capitals. We attempted in Vercelli to distinguish large caps and small caps. Then we ran a very short reliability study and found that maybe sixty per cent of the time we would agree on what was a small cap and what was a large cap. With that we eliminated the distinction. There are capitals and then there are lower case letters. All of the encoding of non-linear items such as superscripts and expansions is done at the end of the word. It does look a little messy on the page, but we are hoping eventually to run this through a program for printing that will restore the brackets around restorations and italicize expansions.

The encoding scheme requires that a unique character for each item, like restoration or expansion, be placed adjacent to the final grapheme of the word or graph and after that a number, or series of numbers, to indicate which letter position this particular code refers to. For example, if the first and second letters of the word had been restored, there would be a slash at the end of the word and then '1, 2,' saying that the restored letters are the first and second.

Even with this I don't think we've made any major breakthroughs in running concordances. We began with a key word out of context concordance system that Control Data Corporation has developed for a series of their machines and, by modifying and updating it, made it not like what it had been, and we ended up with something which I can show those of you afterwards who are interested. It prints the key words in darker impressions than the contexts which then follow. This is done very simply by overprinting the key word twice; this is very good for visual impressions – I can't say, however, that the whole page is aesthetically pleasing, but it certainly is easier to read than using uniform printing. However, this does create difficulties in trying to collate the tape from our concordance with anybody else's tape, as now instead of just one line for a key word there are three in a row. The extra two lines would have to be deleted, but I'll talk about that a little later when we discuss problems of combining various research efforts. The concordance program also prints at the end of each concordance a list of all key words with their frequencies of occurrence within the given concordance.

The program itself is reasonably flexible, allowing you to input a unit of up to four hundred characters. Now this means that you must include within that four hundred characters the identification of the text – page and line, or whatever other identifiers you wish to have – plus the line or syntactic unit or whatever kind of unit that you wish to deal with. Once you have done this you then can specify whether or not you want a particular word not to be included in the concordance – the so-called stop words. One could either

indicate words not to include in the concordance or include a list of words
and say *only* these words should appear in the given concordance. Furthermore, we allow up to one hundred forms to be normalized. That is, if you
want variant spellings of a particular form to be listed under a single form,
you designate the normal form and each variant and the concordance program carries out the proper substitutions for the key words. At some later
date we will consider expanding this facility to handle up to 1,000 or so
normalized forms. The output we obtain goes either directly to a printer
or on to magnetic tape which then can be printed any number of times at
a significantly lower price than rerunning the concordance.

We are considering at present several small changes to the program. One is
the ability to have any collating sequence that one desires. At the present
time this is determined principally by the peculiarities, and they are quite
peculiar, of the computer itself. Those of you who have seen the brief paper
that I circulated earlier know that machines vary in collating sequences – a
problem that we will have to face in one way or another if various projects,
or the outputs from various projects, are to be combined. We are building
into our program therefore the ability to select any desired collating
sequence.

We have also been experimenting with various techniques for producing
computer output. At present we are working with a golfball and heavy-duty
selectric typewriter, trying to find an inexpensive technique for typing out
pages. The Photon process – which produces perhaps the most pleasing page
that one can obtain mechanically – is extremely expensive for anyone who
does not have the largesse of Cornell University Press behind him. I can only
hope that, thanks to the work of Professor Bessinger and Dr Smith, many
university presses will be more anxious to publish aesthetically pleasing
concordances to Old English texts in the future. I must say that I do not
enjoy purchasing photographs of standard printer output – the wavy lines,
the uneven impressions, and so on. The major problem that one faces in
using any kind of golfball technique, as was mentioned by Dr Smith, is that
it is basically unreliable. One must get an extremely well-tuned typewriter
and that is very difficult to do when one is driving the typewriter twenty
hours a day, six days a week (typewriters rest on Sunday at Wisconsin). We
do have one technique that we are looking into that allows us to go directly
from the magnetic tape, which the program emits, into a small device that
runs the typewriter, thus eliminating punch cards, at this stage. This will
eliminate a certain number of errors but certainly not all of them.

We are, in addition to the regular word concordance, also developing a
letter concordance, and I have a short and imperfect example of it. This
concordance operates on the key words generated by the word concordance
along with their frequencies of occurrence. Each letter in a key word,
followed by the next two letters that come after it or blanks, becomes a
separate record in which is included the word itself and its frequency of

occurrence. These records are then sorted into alphabetical order so that, for example, if one is interested in all of the k-graphs in the Rushworth Matthew he turns to the k section in the letter concordance and there finds – sorted by initial, medial, or final positions within the word – alphabetized lists of the words from the Rushworth Matthew in which the graph k occurs. My basic interest in all of this is Old English orthography and so this concordance is something that I desperately need. I'll show you afterwards an example of this particular concordance.

CROSS   There is one small point which brings up the suggestion that there may be concordances for manuscripts, because one of your people is obviously working from manuscripts with the Vercelli Homilies. What about the nonsense words which occur? Are you going to produce these?

VENEZKY   Yes. Some of the Vercelli Homilies have never been edited, so Professor Erickson really had no choice with some of them.

CROSS   The problem is that for some of these Vercelli sermons there are three or more variant texts in later manuscripts. Is a concordance to a single manuscript going to be useful?

VENEZKY   I would like to reserve judgment on that.

CROSS   But it seems to me to be a waste of time to do a concordance to one text when there are three really.

VENEZKY   Perhaps; we simply did not have the means or the energy when we started. That is, we were interested in the particular text that Professor Erickson had access to, with the hope that we could prove to ourselves that our concording technique was worthwhile. We would consider going on from there.

CROSS   In other words you are using this to learn about computers?

VENEZKY   Well, we are doing two things with this. Professor Erickson is interested in syntax and chose the text to work on for particular syntactic problems. I was interested in perfecting the program for producing concordances and finding out what problems we would run into. We do not have a large budget for this project. Nor do we have any time off to pursue it.

CROSS   I'm not being desperately critical. It's just that I feel that we are playing with this toy, and obviously learning, I admit (and I've learned a lot in the last two days). It would seem perhaps that one can do a little thinking and do something better at the first go. Isn't that true?

VENEZKY   Possibly. I don't want to say that we didn't do any thinking – I really have no other answer. We did consider that and we rejected it as something that would hold the project back for too long.

STANLEY   I was going to ask you simply whether you compared the concordance you produced with Schulte's concordance for Rushworth I that goes over the same ground.[1] I want to hear the kind of additional material which I imagine you would get. Schulte is very complete but I don't think it is quite complete. Has it been compared at all?

1   E. Schulte, *Glossar zu Farmans Anteil an der Rushworth-Glosse* (Bonn, 1904).

VENEZKY   No, actually, the final run on Rushworth has not been done. I made a preliminary run and found a large number of keypunch errors that I had
missed originally, and became quite depressed over all that. I decided
therefore to recycle.

STANLEY   Depression and the making of concordances go together. May I ask you a
question about the Latin, the relationship of the Latin to the Old English
in the Rushworth Gospels? I presume your concordance is one word of
Old English for one word of Latin. Is that right?

VENEZKY   Not quite. There are a number of gaps in the glosses. But I do not include
the Latin, just the Old English.

STANLEY   Oh, Latin is not included? I see.

COLLINS   When you speak of the access to the Vercelli manuscript, is this thing done
from the facsimile or another photographic reproduction, or has Mr Erickson actually gone to the manuscript, and checked dubious readings?

VENEZKY   He spent about a month there and then used the facsimiles.

STANLEY   Max Förster's?

VENEZKY   Yes.

BESSINGER   Professor Venezky, is there some way of getting into the record, on the tape,
and into the open air of this charming room, some of the information in the
splendid paper which you presented?

CAMERON   Yes, we are going to deal with that at the conclusion of this session.

BESSINGER   Internal collation sequences and all, because an Old English materials centre
is going to have to face these matters, and you have raised them so lucidly
here that it would be a great shame if we didn't start thinking about them
soon.

CAMERON   Yes, at the completion of the reports on specific projects we are going to
deal with Professor Venezky's paper.

BESSINGER   Splendid.

ROBERSON   I get the impression that the line number is an integral part of the data given
to the computer.

VENEZKY   Yes.

ROBERSON   Is it really necessary that you prepare the data count-wise?

VENEZKY   It depends upon the physical nature of the text you are dealing with, and
upon the concordance program. If you cannot determine by simply counting
characters which words go on which lines, then it is a necessity if you wish
to identify a particular entry in the concordance by line number.

ROBERSON   But if you had the keypuncher indicate end-of-line?

VENEZKY   Yes, that's another possibility. The factor which is important for us in giving
line numbers is very simply that the concordance program is not at this time
set up to recognize an end-of-line mark and then to substitute some running
tally.

ROBERSON   You would agree, then, that it might be an advantage?

VENEZKY   *Probably.* It does increase computing time. And one would have to ask, at *x*
dollars per hour, what does it cost to do it that way against the cost of key-

punching the actual line numbers. There are problems in dealing with prose
texts in terms of what you take as the unit for listing a particular entry. In
some of these texts it may be convenient to mark units with a special
character and then have the program that processes the text scan for the
unit breaks before forming the concordance.

CAMERON   Now we'd like to turn to Professor Pillsbury of Eastern Michigan University.
Professor Pillsbury has been working on a concordance to the West Saxon
Gospels.

PILLSBURY   I would like very much to second Professor Venezky's remarks about the
cordiality of our reception here. Coming from a rather austere United
States state institution, I feel as if I'm positively spoiled here; but I love it.

My interest in the preparation of concordances to Old English prose texts
is an out-growth of a long-standing concern with the application of descriptive techniques to Old English syntax.[2] Systematic descriptive statements
about historical stages of a language depend upon intimate and exhaustive
knowledge of the texts involved. This intimacy is usually gained through
the laborious accumulation of a prodigious number of citation slips citing
all the syntactic patterns to be considered in the grammatical analysis. The
accumulation of such a treasure of citations is wearying and, considering
the present state of Old English syntactic studies, apparently disheartening
to large numbers of scholars.

A concordance, however, if formatted along appropriate lines and if complete in scope, can shorten this mind-wearying labour tremendously. A
concordance is, in effect, a master catalogue to all the forms in the text upon
which it is based. Furthermore, through the form classes, the user has an
index to various class correlations – agreement, concord, government, reference, etc. In presenting exhaustive information about both the form classes
in the text and their correlative behaviour, the concordance provides its user
with an information retrieval system about the grammatical system of the
text of considerable breadth and depth.

The pre-editing stage of the West Saxon Gospel concordance project has
been carried forward at Eastern Michigan University Instructional Computer

2 Work on the West Saxon Gospel Concordance has been supported by a sabbatical
leave from Eastern Michigan University during the academic year 1967-68. Donald
F. Drummond, the dean of Arts and Sciences, has aided the work of the project
with funds for travel to scholarly meetings and for various essential research
materials. A grant from the Bureau of Research of the Department of Education
enabled the editor to devote a full year to preliminary organization and the establishment of basic editorial procedures. A timely grant from the American Philosophical Society defrayed the unscheduled cost of program translation.

Service. Program translation, debugging, and trial runs of the concordance were performed at the University of Michigan Computer Center using the IBM 360 model 67. Early in the fall of 1967 the Michigan Computer Center shifted from the IBM 7090 to the 360 with time-sharing feature. Welcome as the larger storage space, the faster operation, and the time-sharing feature were, the change also necessitated a complete program translation from 7090 compatible machine language into the G dialect of Fortran and 360 machine assembly language. This work was under the direction of Charles Peck of the University of Michigan Phonetics Laboratory, a most gifted intermediary between man and machine. His fluency in the various machine languages and all their genetic, regional, and social dialects is prodigious.

By Christmas the program was debugged and the not-so-friendly blue giant grudgingly yielded up a trial-run concordance to 1,100 pre-edited lines out of the approximately 5,500 lines of the complete gospel text. For purposes of establishing projections, for either publication or fund-raising, it is convenient to think of this output as a 'subconcordance' of approximately one-fifth of the eventual concordance output. The December subconcordance ran to a total printout output of 670 pages, prefiguring a complete concordance of something like 3,350 printout pages.

The concordance generating program used on the project was Tricon, devised as one of a family of three concordance programs by Sydney Lamb (now at Yale) and Laura Gould at the University of California Mechano-linguistics Project.

An editor's initial task in a project of this kind is to devise a transliteration convention for representing his natural language on a continuous run of IBM cards according to the resources of the 029 keypunch keyboard. During the pre-editing stage, and again in the final printout, a simple graphic accommodation was employed to designate the capital letters of the gospel text and the Old English graphs, ash, eth, and thorn.

	IBM KEYPUNCH KEY-
GRUNBERG'S EDITION	BOARD REPRESENTATION
a	A
æ	A,
d	D
ð	D,
t	T
þ	T,

Three archaic Old English graphemes also occur as capitals, although Æ is infrequent.

any capital	+ plus the letter
Æ t	+ A,T
Ð a	+ D,A
þ y s	+ T,YS
eornostlice	EORNOSTLICE
Eornostlice	+ EORNOSTLICE
EORNOSTlice	+E+O+R+N+O+S+TLICE

There are phonological criteria to support this association of graphs. Historical phonologists assume that both Old English /æ/ and /a/ were neighbouring low vowels. The traditional glossarial and lexicographical editing practice has been to intersperse the listing of ash-initial words within the section of *a*-initial words. The lexicographers Bosworth-Toller, Clark Hall, and Sweet agree in using the alphabetic sequencing *ad-*, *æ-*, *af-*. So do such editors of grammars as Campbell, Moore and Knott, Mossé, Quirk and Wrenn, and the Wrights. Only Holthausen, in his etymological dictionary, lists ash as a separate alphabetic entity following the *a*-listings.

My practice in alphabetic sequencing follows Holthausen's minority practice, since I have been more influenced by modern phonological theory than by traditional lexicographical practice. The sequencing I have used is *a*, ash, *b*, etc.

Old English scribes were not systematic in their use of the consonant pair eth and thorn; either graph could represent either the voiced or the voiceless allophone. In editing, therefore, it seems quite superfluous to sort on both of these symbols, particularly since Old English words began with the voiceless allophone. So, for sorting purposes the two characters have been reduced to one (in the sorting operation only) with all eth/thorn-initial words being referred to a canonical main entry spelled with initial thorn. As a group, these words are sequenced after the *t*-initial words, following a considerable lexicographical practice and because the grapho-phonemic association of *t* and thorn (both being phonetically similar as to point of articulation and voicelessness) seems more apposite than an association with *d* or a position after *z*. In the actual text citation under the main entries, however, words are spelled with the initial graph which they have in the Cambridge manuscript and the Grünberg edition.[3]

Three other symbols were used in pre-editing to establish the textual status of emended forms. These symbols are the parentheses, the virgules or slashes, and the asterisk. Where Grünberg deleted or substituted a form, I have restored the original form between virgules. Beside this form, I have cited her emendations in parentheses. Also, I have followed her practice of indicating conjectural forms or forms without direct precedent in any of the MSS with a preposed asterisk. (See appendix A, p. 55).

Thus, the reader of the concordance will have at his disposal both the scribal readings of the MS, through my indicated restorations, and the related readings of Grünberg's received text. In conclusion, any form which is unmarked in this concordance coincides both with the manuscript and the text version. A form enclosed in parentheses represents an editorial emendation, usually on the basis of parallel texts. A form enclosed in slashes represents a manuscript form rejected from the printed edition but described in the appendixed notes. A form prefixed by an asterisk is a conjectural form necessitated by clarity or logic.

Approaching the gospel text as a linguistic document, I have worked with

3 M. Grünberg, *The West Saxon Gospels* (Amsterdam, 1967).

slightly different aims and assumptions than Miss Grünberg has. I have
generally preferred the reading of the unique manuscript over the various
variants. However, my general preference for the reading of the Cambridge
manuscript is in no wise to be taken as a reflection on Grünberg's editorial
practice or her scholarly acumen; for both I have the highest regard. She
has done invaluable service to Old English studies in providing us with a
scholarly text of one of the best prose documents of its period.

But, for linguistic investigation, scholars have a strong preference for the
reading of the manuscript original, as closely as it can be ascertained. The
actual usage of the scribe – including his idiosyncrasies and even his lapses
or aberrations – is of primary concern for the scholar of language and of
greater value than the possession of a normalized or standardized version
of the text. Indeed, there is the real possibility, for the linguistic scholar,
that normalization will obscure or conceal features about the scribe's
language which may be the very object of the investigation. In short, normalization may have an aheuristic effect for investigators of historical
language.

Most concordances order their main entries in a simple alphabetical order,
without regard to morphophonemic, paradigmatic, or other possible options
for ordering. Cruden's Bible concordance[4] is typical in this respect. The
entries 'love,' 'loved,' 'lovely,' 'lover,' 'lovers,' 'love's,' 'loves' are listed in
strict alphabetic order. The entries 'love' and 'loves' (noun-verb) are un-
differentiated as to part of speech. The noun 'love' is separated from the
paradigmatically related 'love's.' Furthermore, the entries 'go' and 'went,'
as well as 'am,' 'are,' 'be,' 'is,' 'was,' and 'were' are dispersed throughout the
appropriate initial-letter sections without regard to paradigmatic association.

In this concordance, however, morphophonemic and paradigmatic sub-
ordering will override strict alphabetization. One base form from a paradigmatic set is established as the canonical main entry for that type, to which
every token of that type in the corpus may be addressed or referred. The
Old English verb 'beon,' for example, exhibits an unusually high incidence
of base alternation: 'beo-,' 'by-,' 'eart#,' 'eom#,' 'sig#,' 'sy-,' 'synd#,'
'wæs#,' 'wær-,' and 'ys#.' But any inflected token from this set, in context,
can be automatically referred to and subordered under the main canonical
entry BEO-. (The program will also allow for the entry of cross-references
in the main concordance list from non-canonical members of the paradigmatic set to the canonical one, so that the user of the concordance will not
inadvertently overlook forms of the paradigm because they have been alpha-
betically disarranged and his recollection of the inflection of a particular
Old English word momentarily lets him down.)

There are four structural types of canonical main entries in Old English.

---

4   Alexander Cruden, *Cruden's Complete Concordance to the Old and New Testaments;
with Notes and Biblical Proper Names under one Alphabetical Arrangement*, C. H.
Irwin, A. D. Adams, S. A. Waters, eds. (London, 1941).

One canonical type is identical in form with the tokens it represents in the natural-language text. These are the uninflected function words, using Fries' designation for them: words like 'and,' 'in,' 'þe,' 'þonne,' 'swa,' 'witodlice,' etc.

A second class of canonical forms consists of the inflected words both with and without base alternation. The tokens 'sun-u,' 'sun-a,' and 'sun-um' are gathered under the form SUN- ... The set 'broþer#,' 'breþer,' 'breþer#' are listed under BROT,ER- ... The set 'se,' 'þa-(m),' 'þæ-(s),' 'þo-(ne)' is addressed to SE- ... Similarly, the set 'ic#,' 'me#,' 'myn-(#),' 'myn-(es),' etc. is referred to IC- ...

A third class of canonical forms is made up of items composed of strings of separate morphemes functioning as a single unit on the lexemic stratum. These are such recurrent strings as 'oþ þæt,' 'swa hwæt swa,' 'swa þeah,' etc. (canonical main entries OT,-T,A,T; SWA-HWA,T-SWA; SWA-T,EAH). Though morphemically complex, their function is tagmemically singular. The analysis of these items as single units is even ratified on an intuitive native-speaker basis by the fairly common scribal practice of writing these items as units: 'oþþæt,' 'swahwætswa,' 'swaþeah.'

A fourth class contains units which are a combination of our second and third classes. The members of the class are word-phrase units which contain at least one inflectible item. Canonical forms for members of this class are given with the canonical form of the inflectible entry. Thus, the address of the set 'seþe,' 'þone þe,' 'þæsþe,' and 'þamþe' is SE-T,E.

The Old English negative contracted forms like 'neom,' 'nolde,' 'nyste,' etc., have been concorded twice since they represent a fusion of grammatical entities: NE plus the respective verb base. Hence, 'nolde' will be concorded both under NE-A1 for one fused member and under the verb or verb auxiliary base WYLL-VM21A. (See appendix B, pp. 55-6, for notation.)

The problem of homonymy is a constant plague to concordance editors and lexicographers. The Old English token 'hym' is a potential submember of three different inflectional sets which here are canonically and separately addressed as HE, HYT, and HIG. It is to be noted that parsing different tokens of the type 'hym' cuts across gender and number classes within the over-all pronoun paradigm to which these tokens belong. The token 'þysum,' like 'he,' cuts across number forms in the sets of T, AS; T,ES; T,YS. The co-occurrence of like forms in different paradigmatic sets is automatically sorted out in the pre-editing stage by the part-of-speech letter code attached to the form. (See appendix B, pp. 55-6).

To achieve the kind of syntactically and paradigmatically subordered concordance order which was desired for this work, the Tricon program requires the preparation of two exactly parallel sets of IBM cards. One series, the A line, contains the transliterated copy of the text of the gospels including the punctuation and capitalization as reproduced in Grünberg's edition. The program also requires the preparation of a second or B card-run. Cards in the B line must contain exactly the same number of items as the corresponding cards in the A line. For every word of the West Saxon gospel text in the A run, there must be a parallel canonical or main entry form in the B run. In addition, the canonical form is always accompanied by the parsing sort key.

The classification of parts of speech in many language descriptions rests on a weak epistemological base. Either the part of speech definitions contradict the basic theoretical dictum that a grammar should be a self-contained system or else the definitions commit the fallacies of extra-systematic appeal and resort to circularity.

Modern linguists have tried in a variety of ingenious ways to overcome the theoretical weaknesses of extra-systematic appeals and definatory circularity. These efforts usually add up to an attempt to define classes on the basis of *form,* that is, derivational set membership and inflectional set membership, and *function,* that is, potential roles in syntactic strings: subject function, object function, various verbal functions, modification functions, etc.

While the form-function type of definition may overcome the aforementioned epistemological defects, it is very apt to conflict with a third general criterion of grammatical theory, the principle that the best grammatical statement is the simplest or the most concise. It seems to be a fact that writers of grammars will be frequently caught between the horns of a dilemma, one labelled *self-consistency* and the other *simplicity.*

But regardless of the theoretical problems underlying a natural-language parsing system, it is a most useful device in the internal operations of concordance editions. The purpose of a parsing system, as mentioned earlier, is to reduce a part-of-speech classification system to convenient code for the purpose of labelling items in a string according to their functional role. And this corresponds precisely to the needs of the concordance editor in the pre-editing stage of his operation when he must classify the successive tokens in the text according to their form and subclassify according to their syntactic functions.

For the needs of the present concordance in Tricon format, Old English parts of speech have been economically gathered into six superclasses:

1 *nominals,* comprising nouns and all their syntactic replacements (definite pronouns, indefinite pronouns, relative pronouns, etc.); in other words, all items which can function as subjects, objects, and vocatives;
2 *nominal modifiers,* consisting of all the internal constituent orders of noun modifiers within the noun phrase and predicatival noun modifiers;
3 *verbals,* including main verbs in verb phrases and various classes of verbal auxiliaries or other verbal expansion items;
4 *verbal modifiers,* including adverbs;
5 *sentence modifiers,* including various adverb-like particles in modifying relationship to the clause (rather than to individual nouns or verbs in the clause);
6 *clause adjuncts,* comprising various items which embed one clause in an-

other or conjoin clauses.

In addition there is a seventh class, a miscellaneous group of *greetings and exclamations.*

The parsing sort code, which always appears to the right of the hyphen after the canonical main entry heading, consists of a string of letters and numbers in various combinations. All codes begin with a letter or two letters and possible succeeding numbers and letters. The leftmost letter symbolizes the part-of-speech classification. Succeeding letters and numbers signal a variety of subclassifications in the inflected parts of speech: tagmemic role, case, and number in all the nominals; tense-mood, number, and person in the verbs; and tagmemic role, location, number, and categorical identification of the headword in the nominal modifiers. (A sample outline of the modifier subsort is exemplified in appendix C, pp. 56-7).

At this point I would like to turn from basic procedural matters and purely housekeeping affairs to what might be called some broader implication of concordance-making – or 'bare bias.'

Concordances are usually restricted by type or token, or both. In other words, the editor will, for the sake of economy, exclude a list of 'common words of high frequency' from the listing; or he will arbitrarily restrict the number of citations for any type of a pre-set number, so that no type is listed more than fifteen, twenty, or twenty-five times, regardless of the number of actual occurrences of that type in the text.

Although the economic motive for such restrictions is understandable, they directly reduce the effectiveness of the concordance as a scholarly aid in language study for several reasons. In the first place, the highly recurrent function words – the articles, the prepositions, the pronouns, etc. – although they may not seen very exciting or important to the literary or semantic scholar, are exactly the forms which have the most interesting implications for the analyst of descriptive or historical morphology and syntax. No study of Old English noun inflection, for example, can proceed very far or very soundly if preposition citations are disallowed. Furthermore, there is the element of fortuitous discovery in examining any text: a writer may demonstrate important variations in his linguistic system. If an individual preposition is listed for an arbitrary twenty times only, it may well be the case that those twenty citations will all show the preposition governing the accusative case. But perhaps the excluded twenty-first citation – or citations fifty-eight through seventy-four – would show that the same preposition also occurs with dative or genitive inflectional endings.

Old English scholarship is much in need of the kind of encouragement which well-made concordances would provide, especially in the area of syntactic studies. A glance through Fred Robinson's estimable yearly bibliographical compilation bears this out. In a bibliography of somewhat over twenty pages a year, approximately one page of items occurs under the general rubric of linguistics and a number of these listings deal with individual semantic items or with morphological studies. What is conspicuously lacking are titles of systematic analyses of Old English prose, and, considering the ferment stirred up in syntactic analysis by the transformationalists in recent years, the number of such studies seems unduly small.

It is still true, however, that the syntactic scholar is faced with the prospect of having to fill all those shoe boxes with citation slips, unless some mechanical method can foreshorten this chore for him. And probably the linguistic Sears Roebuck catalogue is the most feasible way of accomplishing this saving in labour. When such compendia are finally available on library reference shelves, thanks to the electronic computer, scholars may be encouraged to undertake with interest and enthusiasm a variety of problems in grammar, vocabulary, imagery, or rhetoric from which they are ordinarily discouraged by the brute labour of gathering the data.

APPENDIX A: ST. MATTHEW'S GOSPEL, LL. 257-60: TEXT SAMPLE

257 hig standende on gesamnungum. 7 on stræta hyrnum þæt men hig ge-
258 seon. Soð ic secge eow hig onfengon heora mede. þu soðlice þænne
259 þu ðe gebidde. gang into þinum∗bedclyfan 7 þinre dura belocenre.
260 bide þinne fæder on diglum. 7 þin fæder þe gesihð on diglum he

— —

1 Material occuring in the Corpus manuscript, but deleted from the concordance: /HEDCLYFAN/ cf. line 259
2 Editorial additions or corrections: (H)YRNUM cf. line 257
3 Conjectural forms signalled by the editor: (∗BEDCLYFAN) cf. line 259

APPENDIX B: SIMPLIFIED PARSING CODE KEY

A1 predicate modifier
A2 sentence modifier
AQ interrogative adverb
C1 conjunction, intra nominals
C10 conjunction, intra prepositional phrases
C11 conjunction, intra verbal particles
C3 conjunction, intra noun modifiers ('adjectives')
C4 conjunction, intra 'adverbs'
C5 conjunction, intra clauses
C6 first correlative conjunction
C7 second correlative conjunction
D   definite noun substitute ('personal pronoun,' i.e., third person, singular and plural)
I   indefinite noun substitutes
IA adverb intensifier
IM modifier intensifier
M   (nominal) modifier
P1 preposition, object postposed
P2 preposition, object preposed
PR noun substitute person indicators ('personal pronouns,' i.e., first and second

persons)
Q   interrogative noun substitutes
R   relative noun substitutes
R6   first correlative substitutes
R7   second correlative substitutes
RQ   relative interrogative (modifier)
S1   (clause) subordinator
S6   first correlative subordinator
S7   second correlative subordinator
V   main verb of the clause
VA   verbal auxiliaries
VM   modals
VP1,2   perfect participle
VP3,4   progressive participle
VP5   infinitive, -*an*
VP6   infinitive, -*(a)nne*
VP7   *to*
VV   adverbial verbal
VVP   adverbial verbal, perfect
X   greetings and exclamations

APPENDIX C: MODIFIER SUBSORT CODE

Preposed Modifiers	Postposed Modifiers
1 M01, 02	03, 04 ...

a   quantifiers: 'eall,' 'manig,' 'sum,' etc.
b   pre-article possessives: 'heora,' 'hys,' 'myn,' etc.
c   articles: 'se,' 'þas,' 'þone,' etc.
d   post-article possessives: same set as b.
e   cardinal numbers
f   'oþer'
g   primary ('strong') adjectives

| 2   M11, 12 | 13, 14 ... |

secondary ('weak') adjectives, including ordinal numbers

| 3   M51, 52 ... | |

adjectival complements of verb, 'beon,' 'weorþan'

| 4   MQ01, 02 ... | |

interrogative modifiers: 'hwæs,' etc.

| 5   MR01, 02 ... | |

relative modifiers: 'þæs,' 'þære,' etc.

| 6   MN01, 02 | 03, 04 ... |

titles of rank

| 7   MN11, 12 | 13, 14 ... |

noun possessives

| 8   MN21, 22 | 23, 24 ... |

appositives of headwords in N phrases

HATCH I would be interested to know in tabulating the various case forms you've found, say, following prepositions, what you did in the case of ambiguous forms where it could be more than one case you were dealing with? In many instances this would happen. How did you determine what case it was in any particular instance?

PILLSBURY Well, actually it doesn't work down to a case classification. It works down to a grammatical role classification so that the object of a preposition is classified as N91. Now it may well be that you have an accusative on that list, or it may be that you get a genitive. If the editor or scribe varies his practice here, it simply shows up under the N91 listing. Or you just go down the list for a given noun and it turns up genitive. You record it that way. And you can do the quantification, because the data are listed right there.

HATCH In some cases you must not know even with your list, what case you are actually dealing with.

PILLSBURY In the case of the homonymous case forms you are up against the problem that you are always up against with homonymous case forms. The ubiquitous *e* is not much help to you. This does nothing more than show you the ubiquitous *e*.

MITCHELL If I could ask you a question, I hope it won't seem a brash one. I'm very interested in syntax myself, and as I see it, at the age I'm at, I'm interested in doing something about it, and I'd really like to ask you about the time problem. How long has it taken you to do what you have done with the 1,100 lines, and how much has it cost? If you could give us a rough idea. It doesn't seem a rude question, I mean, it seems a very real one for me.

PILLSBURY Do I undertake this project or not because of what's involved?

MITCHELL I was wondering in a selfish kind of way how much help I could expect to get in my lifetime from these projects. I hope that doesn't seem a rude attitude.

PILLSBURY If anything I have more gray hair than you do. The hard, really serious labour has gone on since October 1967, and this figure is thrown off some because my programmer had to spend all of about nine months in doing a translation job which really isn't attributable to the concordance per se. But eventually it was ready to go and – in a very short time, from Christmas vacation on – we got this output plus another fascicle of equal size. The slow part is your pre-editing or someone's pre-editing, and the pre-editing has taken the same amount of time as the translation.

MITCHELL Your point would be then that the time spent in doing this is repaid at the end, because you can ask so many different questions of the computer once you've got the material.

PILLSBURY And you can ask yourself so many more different questions. As far as money is concerned, the part of this project which was attributable to machine-time for the 670 pages was something in order of between $1,500 and $2,000.

MITCHELL   Thank you very much, thank you.

KEENAN   I have a question about languages. What languages are you using? Do you use Cobol, that sort of thing?

VENEZKY   Our concordance program is written primarily in Fortran but in a variety of Fortran that is difficult to translate from one machine to another for two reasons. First it has statements that are unique to Control Data Fortran, and second, it is heavily dependent upon fitting x number of characters into each machine word, a problem we cannot get around easily. In fact, the concordance program was originally written in a manner that theoretically would allow you to state at the beginning that the machine it was to go on had this number of characters per word, and certain other characteristics, and the program itself would sort of regenerate itself with this in mind. That didn't work. Basically it is Fortran, but a Fortran that is unique for a particular machine.

PILLSBURY   Mine is a G dialect. Is that the latest form of Fortran? No? Well I'm already obsolete. Since we are still in the concordance section of the program, I would like to say something about my bias on the matter of concordance versus lexicon. I am very much committed to the idea that we need the concordance and, if and when the dictionary is done, we will still need concordances to the text as well. I think there is a danger of thinking of the concordances as handmaids or preliminary stages to a dictionary. And I don't think that that is true, much as I want to see the dictionary come into being. I think it is a quite different tool, and even though we may have a superlative dictionary, which I hope we'll have, I'm still going to want concordances to all the Old English texts or manuscripts that I can get my hands on for purposes of dialect comparison, stage comparison, early, late, and that sort of thing.

STANLEY   I was very interested in the range of information your concordance is going to provide, including a great deal of orthographic information. I was wondering whether any attempt has been made to deal with line endings because to some extent the distribution of ð and þ depends in some texts on where the line end falls. Has that been considered at all? If it comes within 'syððan,' for example, or 'oþþe' you might get a different distribution of ð and þ in some manuscripts.

PILLSBURY   If there is a divided word at the end of a line break, I automatically go on to the next line. It is lineated as if it were in the preceding line.

STANLEY   Could one indicate in the concordance that the line ends in the middle – at a particular stage? It would be interesting to do.

PILLSBURY   It would be perfectly feasible, yes. You would just put in some kind of device – a line-break marker instead of the ordinary spacing for a word break.

SMITH   Could I come in on the cost of making a concordance? There are two or three costs that I think we can get an idea of. I think to talk in terms of a penny a word for input is not too far off. It might be a half-cent – it might be two cents – does this seem unreasonable to you?

VENEZKY Are you including the costs of pre-editing?

SMITH No, I am really only talking about putting a text like the *Anglo-Saxon Poetic Records,* as they are printed, into some machine-readable form with no intervention by the scholar except to proofread. I am not talking about any kind of grammatical marking, or even our hyphens which are a much, much simpler thing. I think somewhere in the order of a penny a word may not be too far off.

VENEZKY That is a little high for our work but it's in that range – somewhere between a half-cent and a penny a word.

SMITH I don't know what the running time would be for, say, the Old English – the six volumes of Old English poetry. When we did a crude-looking concordance on the 7094 at IBM it took about fifty-five minutes to concord with a very, very good, fast program, the whole of the six volumes in their un-proofread condition. That's not very much money and computing is getting cheaper all the time, so I think that is the least of our costs. I've got a cost for printing with a Photon composing technique. I don't know where we came up with the figure, but you and I once talked around $3,600 for the Krapp-Dobbie.

BESSINGER For Photon.

SMITH I can't imagine where we got the figure, but I think we got it somewhere once.

BESSINGER Partly from your Photon man, partly from the press, partly from your estimates of words and pages. That's a fairly firm figure.

SMITH Three dollars a page for 1,200 pages, and that's coming down, I understand. The guy we talked to had last year's model and that is why it was cheap – and next year he is going to get this year's model and it will be better and cheaper, or something.

BESSINGER This is a figure compatible with typeset composition. There's no excuse any longer not to have a page that looks as if it had been typeset.

VENEZKY Was he charging you anything extra to create the various Old English letters?

SMITH No, that was going to be very cheap. He might charge $10 per letter, but in the whole picture it was going to be next to nothing. He had a very simple way of doing it; a photographic way. He wasn't etching or doing anything expensive.

VENEZKY They generally program the letters and project them on a high-resolution scope and photograph them one by one. That's how it's composed.

SMITH This was a more directly photographic thing without any scope involved. That is, he had some sort of a glass plate with letters – about 200 letters, I think – in various positions around the plate. He also had a few blank positions on to which new letters could be glued. This is my crude impression of the way it works. Entirely photographic.

MERRILEES I have a simple question for Professor Pillsbury. What if you made a simple, human error in parsing? I don't know any Old English, but I do know some Old French. If you took the word 'que' which has ten or a dozen meanings and it would be quite simple for even the best scholar to make an error in deciding whether 'que' means 'for,' or 'that,' or 'because' or 'which' – have you any retrieval system or correction system.

PILLSBURY   In the first place, I would agree with you; it is a very easy thing to do; it happens every day. I have found that it is economical, I think, and definitely so for time and energy, to let the system, the program, and the printout help you as much as possible; and they do, particularly when you are operating with KWIC format. It is very quick (no pun intended) to see the errors which you have made, so that you don't spend any time reading cards – it's all in the printout, and if errors come out they will be visible and they will be exposed very quickly because you simply 'eyeball' down the centre of the page and here's something which doesn't have the right tag on it, or here's a form which obviously doesn't belong in this set because of shape and everything else. You can do your correcting and you can use the mechanics to help you in doing proofreading.

CLEMOES   I just wanted to ask Professor Pillsbury how he handled word division. Did you attempt to follow the practice of the manuscripts in this respect?

PILLSBURY   No, I overrode it completely.

CLEMOES   You feel it's not really possible to cope with the evidence the manuscript provides in that?

PILLSBURY   I followed Grünberg's text in this.

CLEMOES   Because it was the practical thing to do?

PILLSBURY   It was the practical thing to do. And as I've indicated, I didn't mark the ends of lines because I didn't think it was important to do it.

F. ROBINSON   Concerning the concordance as part of the dictionary project, one thing that we are agreed on here, I think, is that we do need a concordance of all Old English before beginning a dictionary, whatever kind of concordance that may be. And it seems that such a concordance will require a lot of people doing a lot of work. I wonder what your and Mr Venezky's opinions would be about the prospects of getting people with your kind of expertise and experience to join in the labour, both of planning the general concordance project and of working on actual portions of this vast amount of concording which needs to be done?

PILLSBURY   Perhaps a not entirely flippant answer would be, 'What else are we good for?'

CAMERON   Could we move on and have the final report from Walter Bak? Professor Venezky's paper, 'The Computer processing of Old English texts,' deals very much with this sort of question and we will have a full discussion of it to round off the session.

Mr Bak is working at the Centre for Medieval Studies at the University of Toronto, and he has been experimenting with concordances using both manuscript facsimiles and editions. For the purposes of this particular meeting we have gone one step further and experimented with a concordance of an unedited text in Corpus Christi College, Cambridge, manuscript 303.

BAK   My main concerns in computer work have dealt with method. In 1965 I made my first concordance, to Robert D. Stevick, *One Hundred Middle English Lyrics* (Indianapolis, 1964) in order to aid in writing a term paper on imagery. (I said out loud one day 'I wish I had a concordance to make writing this paper easier' and someone asked me 'Well, why don't you make one?') It was useful for what I needed it for but, because it was based on a normalized edition, I decided later that it would not be very helpful for studying the language. Next I tried a concordance to an Old English text. Again, as part of a course, I prepared a concordance to the four signed poems of Cynewulf, basing these on the standard edition in the *Anglo-Saxon Poetic Records*. This one turned out satisfactorily again for what I needed it for. I found it very awkward to use, however, because the occurring forms of any one word would be scattered throughout the concordance; whether the variation in the form is due to the paradigm or dialect or whatever reason, it is, I found, very inconvenient to use the format in which each form of a word is given a separate entry.

This past year, while taking an Old English philology course, I have become more concerned about how the actual Old English manuscript reads. What is the form that is found there? My present plan for concording, therefore, involves a completely different approach, *an approach based on the manuscript readings but also with reference to what is considered the standard edition.* This plan has a twofold advantage because first, it is based on the manuscript which will never change, and second, it takes advantage of the scholarship that has gone into the edition.

What follows is mainly my plan of how to get the manuscript into computer-readable form. I have adopted different symbols with which to work; since this plan is still in the embryonic stage of development, any of these proposed symbols may be changed.

Special symbols are needed for the characters þ, ð, æ, and Þ. (For the time being I just normalize them in my own experimentation.) Special symbols for the 'hooked *e*' and for the ampersand and, perhaps, for the *œ* combination should also be used.

When handling word-division in the manuscript, if what we consider one word is split in two for some reason in the manuscript, these parts are joined together with a hyphen to make the citation easier to read. If two words are connected together in the manuscript, they are separated with a slash to show that they are written together in the manuscript but are commonly read or interpreted as two separate words.

To indicate that a word is split at the end of one line and continued on another line a double hyphen (which looks like an equals sign) is used; the position of the word in the line is now made clear. An end-of-line symbol should also be included. At times this has to be an arbitrary decision since it is not always clear whether the scribe intended one word or two words; each word has to be judged according to its particular appearance, the letters within the word, and that word in relationship to other words.

Regarding punctuation, I have adopted the simple plan whereby a single point in the manuscript is indicated by a period; any other type of punctuation is indicated by a comma. A more complex system than this may prove desirable.

Abbreviations in the manuscript are not expanded because the expansions may be found in the reference to the edition. In order to indicate an abbreviation, however, a period is placed directly after the occurring letters. When the period is used as punctuation, it is preceded and followed by a space on either side to distinguish the two usages of the period.

Accent has not been taken into consideration.

Capitalization has been ignored for the time being.

Parentheses are used to indicate what I call a 'tampered text,' meaning that, if a letter is obviously written over an erasure, that letter is enclosed in parentheses to show that it was not what was originally in the manuscript. It was put in at some other time.

Likewise, if there is an erasure and nothing else was added, empty parentheses are used to indicate that an erasure was made but nothing else had been put in.

If there is a loss in the manuscript – for instance, in *Beowulf* something might have been burned away at the edge of a folio – whatever letters are left are immediately followed by a plus sign to show there was more to the word but that there has been some sort of damage (fire, worm holes, or whatever). There is nothing there now and I cannot say what was there, if it's not there. I'm not trying to edit it. Instead of trying to make that decision from the manuscript I would provide the editor's opinion from the standard edition.

Carets with points at the sides are used for glosses or for additions at another time, whether they are above the line or in the margin or whatever. For example, in the Preface to the *Pastoral Care* in Hatton 20, for the word 'weorold,' the *d* is added above the line and that *d* would be included in these carets to show it was not originally written as part of the word but that it was added at another time. I do not try to make a distinction between contemporary or later additions; I merely try to distinguish additions from the original.

A question mark is used wherever there is a doubtful reading of the manuscript, or when there is uncertainty as to the actual reading of the manuscript. This is my way of indicating that I am open to suggestions and willing to change my reading.

The form of the reference for the manuscript being concorded is letter K (for the Ker *Catalogue*) plus the number of the manuscript in the catalogue; folio number plus R for recto, V for verso; line number.

An A locates a word above the line; for example, 11A would mean that word was located above line 11. A B locates a word below the line, L in the left margin or to the left of the body of writing, R to the right margin, H at the head of the page or folio, F at the foot of the page or folio. In this way one would know exactly where any certain word is located on the page in the manuscript.

The 'plus' symbol is also used in the reference if a word is split onto two different lines; for example, if a word is on line 5 and continued on line 6, it is indicated by 5 followed by a 'plus' sign – the plus means the next logical number. The 'plus' symbol may also be used in the reference for folios; with 20V+, the next logical place is 21R. If a word were split over two different folios one could use a plus with both the folio and the lines.

Symbols are needed to indicate certain circumstances where the edition would differ from the manuscript. (At present I have no definite suggestions as to what these symbols might be.) A symbol should indicate the expansion the editor of the standard edition has made for an abbreviation in the manuscript.

Another symbol is needed to indicate any restorations that have been made by the editor.

Most important of all, emendations which have been suggested by the editor should be given. I would keep the manuscript reading, 'right' or 'wrong,' but I would also give the emendation that the editor had provided. One of the primary reasons behind my decision to *base* my concordance work on the manuscripts and to retain the manuscript reading is that Old English scholars may demonstrate that many of these 'mistakes' in the manuscripts do make sense after all and that no emending is needed.

In general terms, the data which one would punch onto cards (I will talk in terms of punched cards rather than any other technique) would be, first, the text of the manuscript, a line-by-line arrangement as that of manuscript. The division would be a line of the manuscript. Folio and line reference number would be given. From that, to work with each word, a separate program would generate a separate card for each word of text for two important reasons. Because I found the Cynewulf concordance so cumbersome, I prefer to have a concordance based on normalized headwords as in a dictionary, so that the word one is looking up can be looked for in one place and with all its variant forms there, regardless of the reason for those variations, paradigm or dialect or whatever. Complete cross-references can be provided from manuscript readings to the normalized headwords so that, if someone were unsure what the normalized spelling is, this information would be provided as a cross-reference. For the time being, since I am working on Hatton 20 which is in early West Saxon I am using F. Holthausen, *Altenglisches etymologisches Wörterbuch* (Heidelberg, 1963) as the basis for the normalized spelling. The page and line references for the standard edition would be added to the card. Then one could add such information as the expansions

restorations, and emendations. One could also add parts of speech or syntactic functions at this stage if this information would be needed later.

The resulting output would include the text printed out as a diplomatic
transcription of the manuscript. That text would be printed out preceding
the concordance to aid anyone in doubt about the interpretation of a certain
reading of the manuscript. Next the concordance itself would follow. The
form of each entry would be, first, the normalized headword; this would be
followed by the frequency count of all forms of that headword and, in a
horizontal list, an alphabetic listing of all the occurring forms with the individual frequencies. This arrangement would make for a more convenient
comparison of individual forms. The list of forms with frequencies would
be followed by a listing of the restored readings and emendations that were
made in the edition. The citation from the text is provided next. I prefer
having the citations based on what I call 'sense-units' rather than syntactic
units or a space limit. A 'sense-unit' is the smallest amount of text read by
itself. This could be a whole sentence, it could be a clause, or it could be
just a phrase; but when one reads it there are no extra words or extra letters
added and it will make sense standing on its own. This is something I would
try to keep as short as possible, if only for economic reasons, but different
checks could be worked out. Each citation would have the reference to the
Ker catalogue number and the folio or page in the manuscript (depending
on how it is numbered; that is something that probably should be standardized first, especially if several concordances are going to be merged, to
avoid confusion from two systems of numbering); the line in the manuscript
page or folio; the page and line in the edition; and if necessary the volume
of the edition. Among the headwords would be the cross-references so that
one could find any form that occurs in the manuscript. This would aid not
only in using the concordance as a finished product, but also in case there is
any disagreement about how a form was normalized or in the interpretation
of a word. Appendices I have in mind for my own concordance to Hatton
20 are a frequency list, and a back-word list. Rather than concordances for
separate letters, I have decided on a listing by the first occurring vowel in the
word. Since the stress in simple Old English words is on the first syllable, in
most cases this listing will turn out in effect to be a list of root vowels. Another feature would be a KWIC-index of compounds so that one would know
what prefixes or elements a word combines with within that text. A thesaurus
based on Carl Darling Buck, *A Dictionary of Selected Synonyms in the Principal Indo-European Languages* (Chicago, 1949), would be an added convenience in using the finished product as a concordance.

There are some obvious disadvantages to this method. First of all, it does
involve editing to some degree. Decisions made about sense-units and in
some instances manuscript readings would naturally be open to criticism.
Perhaps the greatest disadvantage is the time to be spent on providing the
normalized headwords; nevertheless, I do think that the benefit of having

all the information under one headword compensates for this time. Another consideration is, should somebody whose field is Old English be spending time keypunching from a manuscript facsimile?

There are, however, great advantages to using a method for making concordances based on the manuscript readings but also with reference to the standard edition. First, references are to the manuscript *and* to the edition; if a new and better edition comes out it is very easy to change the references to the edition since the foundation of the work is the manuscript which will always remain constant. It will be complete for every word in the manuscript and no ghost-forms should appear. In my opinion, this format makes it easier to use for literary studies. Perhaps my main reason for basing such work on manuscripts is one which is never taken into consideration – there is no reason why a concordance, especially one to a medieval text, should not and can not be prepared so that it can be used to study the language as well as the literature. Since the system of cross-references takes care of normalization and emendations, the method provides the exact spellings of the manuscripts and therefore can be used to study phonology and morphology. The form of the resulting data would also be handy for dialect study. Other possible studies are orthography, dating the manuscript, even locating where it had been written. Also a concordance based on the manuscript would aid in preparing a new edition.

This approach is based on the manuscripts, and the manuscripts are the same today as they were 1,000 years ago (unless they were since damaged) and they will still be the same 1,000 years from now – they are constant; editions, however, vary according to the standards in existence when that particular edition was produced.

CAMERON I don't know what to do about questions now because time is running short, and I do want to spend as much time as possible on Mr Venezky's paper, because it sums up what we have been saying here. There is really a fair amount of agreement and, if there are questions, we might have this paper and then go on to questions. I hope that afterwards samples of the concordances people have been working on can be shown at the table at the end of the room and that we may talk with the originators on specific points.

Now, Professor Venezky's paper is entitled 'The computer processing of Old English texts.'

VENEZKY This paper deals with both the computer generation of concordances to Old English texts and the collation of concordances prepared on different machines by different concordance programs. A discussion of the problems involved in these tasks comprises the body of the paper. Appendix A (p. 69) contains proposals for Old English text-processing standards; appendix B (p. 73) presents some of the technical problems encountered in merging magnetic tapes produced on different machines. While the chief motivation for this paper is the proposed (new) Old English dictionary, other fruits of standardized data processing are discussed briefly on pages 68 and 69.

The proposals contained here are intended as a basis for discussion, and not as a definitive scheme. As will be seen in appendix A, several problems have been left unresolved, while others have rather arbitrary solutions.

GUIDELINES FOR STANDARDS

Standards for processing Old English texts should cover two basic areas: (1) the encoding of the text into machine-readable form and (2) the format and medium of storage for both the encoded input and the concordance output. Proposed standards must be applicable to the machines of the major computer manufacturers (IBM, CDC, Univac, and Burroughs), either now in existence or announced for the near future, and be based primarily upon punched-card input and magnetic-tape storage. Such standards, however, should be applicable to other common input procedures (punched paper tape, optical character reading, etc.) or other storage media (disks or paper tape). Throughout this discussion, however, I will assume punched-card input and magnetic-tape storage (of both the images of the original input cards and the output of the concordance).

Text encoding

The encoding of a text involves the translation of the text and all editorial additions into a linear sequence of keypunch symbols. For Old English texts, options exist for the following:

Symbol substitutions

Ash, thorn, eth, and wynn must be replaced by keypunch symbols. Capitals and accent marks must be encoded into a linear sequence with the segmental characters. A special marker and encoding scheme must be devised for the runic alphabet.

Editorial changes

Expansions and restorations must be indicated. If markers for restorations, capitals, etc. are not placed at the end of each word, alphabetizing problems will occur.

Text variants

If similar texts are to be combined into a single concordance, variants must be indicated.

Unit designation

While the *context* for any entry in a poetic concordance is generally the line in which the entry occurs, it is desirable for prose texts to select a syntactically defined unit for the *context*. Since such units are not normally identified in the texts, editorial decisions must be made, based upon the nature of the text and the maximum allowable context size of the concordance program. (Most concordance programs limit the maximum number of characters for any input record.) When the smallest desirable syntactic unit exceeds the maximum allowable unit, as in numerous ambling Latinate texts, an arbitrary cut must be made. Such cuts should be marked so that an editor will be able to identify them.

Page and line numbers
Each input record for a concordance contains a syntactic unit (or partial unit), and text, page, and line designators. If concordances to different texts are to be collated for comparison or dictionary editing, it is imperative that unique identifiers be assigned to each text.[5] Furthermore, it is desirable that all researchers use the same page and line identification schemes. In a text like the Vercelli Book, one can number lines for the homilies from top to bottom – regardless of which homilies are included, or renumbering can begin either at the top of the page or when a new homily begins. Each method provides unique recovery of the original text (assuming that the homily numbers are retained), but one or the other should be adopted as a standard.

Stop words
In preparing a concordance, a researcher can designate that certain words not appear in the concordance. These words, called stop words, are usually high frequency function words. (One can also, with many concordance programs produce a concordance which will list only the words which the researcher indicates.) Whether or not stop words should be used probably should not be the concern of these standards. However, a suggested list of stop words should be available for those who wish to use them. (Some thought should be given to the volume of data that the dictionary editors will face if all texts are concorded without stop words – and to the editors' dilemma if *all* texts are concorded with stop words.)

Programming problems
Several technical problems concerned with concordance programs must be considered if comparability of output is to be attained; these are collating sequence, end stripping, and output format. They are discussed in appendix A.

Storage
If Old English materials in machine-readable form are to be exchanged, then both the input cards and the concordance output should be written on magnetic tape in a format that will ensure maximal compatibility from machine to machine. (A reel of magnetic tape, 2,400 feet in length, can store from 35,000 to 200,000 cards, depending upon the storage technique. The tape costs approximately $16.00.) What must be standardized are: tape labelling (or non-labelling), recording density and parity, blocking factor, and end-

---

5   A variety of abbreviations are being used for Old English texts. For example, *Beowulf* is *B* in Hall, *Beow.* in Campbell, and *Beo. Kmbl.* or *Beo. Th.* in Bosworth-Toller. The most important constraints for data processing are that all abbreviations be composed of upper-case symbols (i.e., numbers, special characters, or upper-case alphabetics) and be unique. (All existing publications mix upper and lower case; e.g., in both Hall and Campbell, *CP* represents King Alfred's translation of Gregory's *Pastoral Care,* while *Cp* stands for the *Corpus Glossary.*)

of-file indicators. A question for future discussion is the non-compatibility between new IBM machines, which record data in eight channels across the width of the tape, and most other machines, which use six channels.

OLD ENGLISH MATERIALS CENTRE

If a large number of concordances are to be made by different persons throughout North America, England, and the Continent, the collecting, storing, and distributing of these materials must be undertaken. Conceivably, this could be left to each individual; however, to guarantee the availability of materials a central agency will be needed. To achieve this, an Old English materials centre should be established at a university which has scholars active in Old English research, computing facilities for producing concordances, and funds to support part of the work. The remainder of the support should be solicited from wherever funds are available: ACLS, Office of Education, NSF, etc. The functions of the centre would be:

1 To collect, catalogue, and distribute Old English texts and concordances in machine-readable forms.

2 To run concordances and other programs for scholars who do not have access to concordance programs at their own universities but can pay for the necessary machine time.

3 To collate on a continuing basis the concordances being produced so that, when the final concordance is run, dictionary editing can begin. (It is not clear at this point what collations of texts will be best for editing – whether there should be one grand concordance to all Old English texts, or various concordances, based upon dialect, date, or other factors. It is clear, however, that some preprocessing of the concordances is a desirable prerequisite to editing.) By the time the editing begins, it may be practical to edit materials by projecting them directly from computer memory onto a remote terminal screen. The editor would work with a light pen (or equivalent) and keyboard, transferring raw data from one side of the screen to a page or column image being composed on the other side, inserting, deleting, and replacing data as he proceeds. Whatever technique is employed, the centre would have to be responsible for proper formatting of data.

4 To prepare (and distribute, when possible) programs for producing concordances and other research materials.

An Old English materials centre should not undertake or sponsor research on Old English language or literature, but should facilitate the research undertaken or contemplated by others through its computer-related activities. It is important that this point be made clear; the centre's basic mission is to aid a certain area of research, not to engage in the research itself. It will hold no monopolies on research topics, nor have any influence over the studies undertaken or the people who undertake them. It is a service centre whose products are in the public domain and whose success depends chiefly upon the co-operation it receives from the people whom it is to benefit.

END PRODUCTS

Once texts are transferred to a machine-readable form, a variety of operations can be performed quickly and inexpensively upon them. While most discussions in the past have centred on concordances since they are needed for dictionary editing, other outputs deserve consideration. Two of these are:

Frequency lists. The concordance program in use at the University of Wisconsin produced with each concordance an alphabetized list of keywords which occur in the concordance, along with the frequency of occurrence of each word. These lists are invaluable for comparing vocabularies.

Letter concordances. For studies of orthography and phonology, a letter concordance is an indispensible aid. This form of concordance lists, for every graph which occurs in a text, the keywords from the concordance in which the graph occurs (usually sorted by position of the graph – initial, medial, final), along with the frequency of occurrence of each word. One could, for example, find immediately the distribution of eth and thorn from such a list. (A letter concordance programme is now being developed at the University of Wisconsin.)

REFERENCES

J. B. Bessinger Jr, *A Short Dictionary of Anglo-Saxon Poetry.* Toronto: University of Toronto Press, 1960

J. Bosworth and T. N. Toller, *An Anglo-Saxon Dictionary.* Oxford: Clarendon Press, 1898

A. Campbell, *Old English Grammar.* Oxford: Oxford University Press, 1959

Richard Cleasby and Gudbrand Vigfusson, *An Icelandic-English Dictionary,* 2nd ed. with suppl. by W. A. Craigie. Oxford: Oxford University Press, 1957

J. R. Clark Hall, *A Concise Anglo-Saxon Dictionary.* 4th ed. with suppl. by H. D. Meritt. Cambridge: Cambridge University Press, 1960

F. Holthausen, *Altenglisches etymologisches Wörterbuch.* Heidelberg: Carl Winter, 1963

John F. Madden and Francis P. Magoun Jr, *A Grouped Frequency Word-List of Anglo-Saxon Poetry.* Cambridge, Mass.: Harvard University, Department of English, 1954

APPENDIX A: TEXT ENCODING

Symbol substitutions

$ ash
+   eth
*   thorn
W   wynn

Non-segmental features and editorial changes

Capitals, accent marks, restorations, and expansions are indicated by the special symbols shown below, placed at the end of the word to which they apply without intervening space.

) Large cap
)) Small cap
≠ Superscript[6]
/ Restoration
= Expansion

The characters to which these codes refer in the encoded word are indicated by numbers which immediately follow the code. These numbers designate the ordinal positions of characters, beginning with the first character as 1. Successive numbers are separated by commas. Inclusive numbers can be shown by the dash notation, e.g., 5-8, or by denumeration, e.g., 5, 6, 7, 8. If more than one code applies to a word, the order of code – plus – number group is insignificant. An initial capital can be indicated by the cap code alone, or by the cap code followed by the number 1. A code which applies to all characters of a word can be indicated by complete or abbreviated denumeration, e.g., 1-4 or 1, 2, 3, 4, or by the letter A.

Substitutions for abbreviations like 7 (for *and*) and for punctuation need further study. The system used for Rushworth I and for Vercelli Homilies is:

Old English form	keypunch symbol
7 (and)	7 (numeric seven)
semi-colon	; (semi-colon)
high point	, (comma)
low point	. (period)

A variant word from another text should be placed in parentheses and located immediately after the word it is a variant of (but separated from it by at least one space). The variant word should have a dash sign suffixed to it, followed immediately by its text, page, and line codes, separated by periods, e.g., (BUTAN-MAT. 9.23). Each variant word should have its own parentheses and code, even if several occur in succession. This coding scheme should be used when variants comprise a small percentage of the input data (less than two per cent). For greater densities of variants, separate concordances should be made.

Runic characters

Each runic character should be assigned a Roman letter. A runic character or character sequence should begin with two diagonals (//) and end with either a space or two additional diagonals. (This latter situation would occur only when a runic character was adjacent to a Roman character.) This system does not apply to runic characters adopted into English orthography.

6 If different forms of superscripts are to be distinguished, different letters (other than A) should be assigned to each. The superscript marker ≠ should be followed immediately by the appropriate letter and then the place indicator. The superscript marker ≠ appears as a single quote mark (') on some keypunches and printers.

Unit designation

If an input unit cannot terminate at an appropriate clause break because of input length limitations, sufficient room should be left for a 'forced termination' indicator, *.n.,* where *n* is a numeral which is unique for each unnaturally split line in a text. The left-over string (or the next segment of the left-over string) should begin with exactly the same indicator so that an editor can easily reconstruct the entire unit from the concordance alone. (An alternative proposal is to repeat the last word of one unit at the beginning of the next unit.)

Page and line numbers

If pagination has not been established, the editor should do so following established procedures. Line numbers should begin with the first line of the text and recycle to one at the top of each succeeding page and at the beginning of separate literary entities (e.g., a new homily). Titles at the top of a page should be assigned line number zero. (An alternate proposal would be to assign 1T.)

Stop words

The computer committee should prepare a tentative stop-word list, based upon available frequency counts. This should be published for comments in the *Old English Newsletter.*

Collating sequences I

Existing dictionaries and word lists display variation in the selection of Old English graphemes and in the alphabetization of what is selected. These problems pertain primarily to æ, þ, ð, and certain infrequently occurring Roman characters (*q, k, x,* and *z*). The positioning of æ in the alphabet is a prime example of collational chaos: Hall (1960) and Bosworth-Toller (1898) treat it like *ae,* and therefore insert it between *ad* and *af*; Holthausen (1934) inserts it after *a,* while Bessinger (1960), following Madden and Magoun (1954), relegates it to the end of the alphabet, after þ which follows *z*. The placements of þ, ð are similarly incompatible. Furthermore, *qu* is typically normalized to *cw, k* to *c,* and þ occasionally to ð (or vice versa). The need for a standard collating sequence is based upon economics – that is, the desire to merge concordances without expensive character conversion and resorting. The need for retaining all existing graphemes is, I hope, also non-controversial. While they may not be desired for the proposed dictionary, they are valuable for orthographic studies and for determining dates of composition and provenance. The costs of retaining the few examples of *qu* and *k,* for example, are rather small under any circumstances, and are minuscule in comparison with the potential rewards.[7] It is recommended, there-

---

7 The justification given for normalizing *k* to *c,* i.e., that they are variants, furthermore is unfounded. In Ru. I, *k* is used only for the sound that remains /k/ in Middle English, never for what becomes /č/. (It can be argued further that in Mercian in prehistoric Old English the palatal and velar variants of Gmc. /k/ are in phonemic contrast.)

fore, that all graphemes be retained: æ, þ, ð, q, etc. (This does not apply to allographic variants, like the Old English forms of s.)

For collating sequences, two basic systems are common: one based upon Scandinavian and the other upon modified Latin. The Scandinavian tradition represented by Bessinger and Madden and Magoun places ð after d (for etymological reasons) and þ, æ after z.[8] The modified Latin tradition places æ in or around the a's, and ð and þ after t.

The recommended sequence then becomes: a, æ, b, c, d, e, f, g, h, i, k, l, m, n, o, p, q, r, s, t, ð, þ, u, v, w, x, y, z[9]

Collating sequences II: *Sorting*

Excedrin headache no. 99 (approaching *grand mal*) results from the lack of a uniform internal collating sequence for all computers. Even within a single manufacturer this sequence varies. The IBM 1401, 1410, 7010, 7040, and 7044 use the BCD Standard Interchange Code (as does Burroughs); in this code, all special characters except one occur before the alphabetics and all the numerals occur after them. On the IBM 7090 and 7094 (and the larger CDC and Univac machines), the numerals occur first, followed by a chaotic interleaving of special characters and alphabetics. On the IBM system/360 yet another sequence is employed, with an extended set of characters.

If concordance programs do not convert character codes to achieve a standard collating sequence, some output tapes will have to be resorted before they are merged with the master file. Sorting is expensive. If it must be done, and if other operations must be performed on the output tape, then consideration should be given to running all concordances with a single concordance program.

End stripping and output format

These standards, if they are to exist, should be proposed by the computer committee after the ramifications of the various alternatives can be studied.

STORAGE

Input records should be on six-channel (seven with parity bit) magnetic tape, recorded in odd parity at a density of 556 bpi. Physical records should be either single-card images, or blocked-card images, with no more than 100 card images per physical record. The entire file should terminate with at least two end-of-file marks.

The concordance output format probably cannot be standardized beyond the formats produced by existing concordance generating programs. This should be considered by the computing committee.

8 For notes on the Icelandic alphabet and its history, see Cleasby and Vigfusson, p. xv.
9 Etymology is reflexive; just as placing ð after d can be based on the development of ð out of d, so can placing ð and þ after t be justified on the basis of their replacement by *th*.

APPENDIX B: TAPE COMPATIBILITY

Under ideal conditions the output tapes for different concordances would be merged without revision into one large concordance. For a number of reasons this will probably not be possible, that is, revision of each output tape will be required before merging. Incompatibilities among existing machines include:

1 Tape size

Some tape units record data in six-bit groups plus a parity bit. Others record in eight-bit groups plus a parity bit. Most campuses have only the six-bit form; others have a six- or eight-bit option; and a few have only the eight-bit variety. (Converters are available for translating from one form to another.)

2 Character codes

The codes written on tape for the alphabet, numerals, and special characters are not identical across all major computers. For example, the Burroughs (B5500) codes for the equal sign, left and right parens, plus sign, and semicolon are different from the CDC, Univac, and IBM (7090 series) codes for these characters. Character conversion will probably have to be done when the tapes are merged, since prior conversion will affect printing.

3 Print format

The output of all existing programs is intended for printing. Consequently, carriage control codes and blank fillers are used to obtain a desired page format. Since it is highly unlikely that the formats produced by any two concordance programs are the same, additional compatibility problems must be resolved. One is that the number of characters per line varies from printer to printer. Some allow 120, others allow 132 or 144. This is not an insurmountable problem for merging tapes from different computing centres, but it does require some programming.

Another problem is that the position of the keyword within the print line will vary from one concordance program to another. Once divergent lines are merged, either the keywords must be in identical (relative) positions, or pointers must be added to each line to indicate where the keyword is located. (This latter scheme is not recommended.)

4 Miscellaneous

Not everything that is written on tape appears on the printed page. For example, the concordance program at the University of Wisconsin prints keywords darker than the remainder of each record by over-printing each keyword twice. Therefore, for every keyword printed, three key-words are transmitted to the printer. (The line eject is suppressed after the first two of the three printings.) For merging into a grand concordance, the extra keywords should be deleted.

Let me say in conclusion that this paper was prepared and distributed as a series of suggestions and not as a definitive scheme – which I hope is clear from the introduction. I felt that there were certain issues that needed to be discussed and for which solutions eventually must be found, and I tried to summarize these in this particular paper. I have taken the attitude that concordances are needed for a variety of reasons; that of course we are all interested in the dictionary and hope that we can begin work soon on it; but that there is also a need to make generally available the work of researchers in this particular area. One could say that we face the chance of creating a class of haves and a class of have-nots, the have-nots being the mechanically deprived who don't have access to computers or concordance-making programs. I say this half jokingly and half seriously. Those who do have access to computers and to concordance programs can in a matter of weeks or months have data that others might have to spend a lifetime accumulating. I think all of us are very anxious to see such materials distributed as widely as possible. To do this we must find solutions to a number of problems. We must first decide what types of materials we would like to distribute. Obviously the concordance itself is the most important object, but many people, I think, would like to have also the initial data (that is, the cards or the card images on tape) that went to make the concordance. Some people want to have other arrangements of the data and possess the programming facilities to make them. More money is spent in preparing the data and transferring it to magnetic tape than in running the concordance. Therefore if materials are already on tape, it is to everyone's advantage to be able to distribute them.

I've tried to outline in the report a number of problems beyond this – that is, beyond deciding what it is we would like to distribute. If we are going to distribute the input data, that is, the actual text in some format, it is desirable that everyone should format his text so that other people can use it conveniently. I don't know if this is possible, however. There are serious problems that involve not only the physical incompatibility of different types of tapes, but also the codes that different computers generate on tape for particular characters. These things I think we can discuss later. The nitty-gritty perhaps of all this will not be of interest to everyone here. As to the concordance, I think, as Professor Bessinger was pointing out, one of the most important problems to discuss is that of collating sequences. Just where will *æ*, *ð*, and *þ* come in the standard alphabetical sequence? Furthermore, it seems that it is important to reach some agreement on symbol substitutions. We are all probably working with the same standard set of keypunch symbols. Probably three years from now we won't be restricted to these things, but I suspect that for the next couple of years we will be. Therefore it seems best to stick to the standard substitutions. For those people who have already made concordances or prepared data that don't use these, I don't think this is going to be a major problem. Someone, perhaps the Old English materials centre, could take on the task of converting non-standard tapes – whether concordance output or the initial input data – to a normal form.

There are a variety of problems other than those I have listed: what to do about editorial changes, text variants, unit designations, page and line numbers, and whether or not to set up a list of standard stop words – a problem which I really don't have much of an opinion on. It has been pointed out here that with the types of studies being undertaken, it is best to include all words that occur in a text. However, I am sure that some people working with rather lengthy texts are going to want to delete certain function words simply because of cost.

On another matter, magnetic tapes today are extremely inexpensive. A tape 2,400 feet in length costs about $16.00, and this price has been falling dramatically over the last year or year and a half. So it is rather inexpensive to distribute materials in machine-readable form. What I suggest we should do is discuss first what kinds of materials should be distributed and then talk about the more important problems such as alphabetizing and symbol substitution. So let me turn the floor back to the chairman for whatever manner of discussion he wishes to set up.

BESSINGER Mr. Chairman. I have strong opinions about this – that is, it doesn't matter twopence what order we use just so we all use the same order. The startling thing that comes out of Professor Venezky's wonderfully lucid paper is the possibilities for inadvertent non-standardization. The opportunities are simply overwhelming because even within the same machine-manufacturer's product the collation sequence order, for example, is different from machine to machine, from model to model. So that people working with the very same IBM machine or Burroughs machine or Univac machine made in a different month or different year may be in fact producing programmatic differences that would bring to a shuddering halt any attempt to merge programs from two different scholars working on the very same texts. This standardization of materials and collaboration and collation of efforts by individual working scholars is, it seems to me, the very first order of business for an Old English materials centre such as I hope will very shortly be established, on the principles outlined here by Professor Venezky.

VENEZKY Are the problems of merging tapes from different projects clear to everyone? Are there questions on this? What we are involved with primarily is cost. If we have two tapes from two different concordance programs that are not compatible, we cannot simply merge them by reading entries from one tape and comparing them to entries on the other and fitting them together in a standard sequence. What we would have to do is take one of the tapes and either completely rerun the concordance or process it in such a way as to put it into the form of the other tape. And this could become extremely expensive. I don't think we would want to incur that cost, if it can be avoided.

BAILEY I just want to endorse this view. For at least the last six or seven years various appeals have been made for standardized text-encoding schemes and yet, as new projects begin, each individual (of course there are the limitations of the particular machine where he happens to be – that is a hard one to beat) sets out blithely to translate his special characters into the standardized keypunch. The decisions made are just different, and for no reason at all. I don't know what can be done here except perhaps, as Professor Venezky has suggested in his paper, to publicize a scheme and make sure people know about it. I'm sure people will be glad to standardize if they know of a good scheme.

SMITH   I am a little confused – I think some of us are talking about encoding of input texts while some of us are talking about the format of output concordances ... In this connection we really, as Professor Venezky commented, all had the same keypunches at our disposal and whereas we used a 7 for þ, Professor Pillsbury, I think, very cleverly used a T,. I can see that your þ is going to collate where you want it to and mine doesn't. But we had the same keypunch. We didn't do it for mechanical reasons – we did it for this arbitrary reason that you pointed out – I mean, we're different for arbitrary reasons and not for good reasons. On the other hand, I am not sure that it is all that serious, that is, how hard is it to convert our þ's to his or vice versa? It's a program and it's machine time, but not a whole lot, or do you think it is a more serious problem than I think it is?

VENEZKY   No, I think it's strictly a matter of cost and convenience. The question is, are we always going to have such large amounts of money around that we can afford to run every concordance twice? Once to use it and once to normalize it so that others can use it.

SMITH   Now you are talking about compatibility of finished concordances.

VENEZKY   Well, actually, I think we should talk about both. I mentioned earlier the desirability of distributing both the input data and the final product.

BESSINGER   Are there not three things to talk about, excuse me: compatibility of encoding, compatibility of storage, and the compatibility of output; all three are going to be expensive if they needlessly duplicate or generate varieties, dialects, of machine languages and so on and so on, that over the long run are simply not necessary.

VENEZKY   The physical problems of storage we can handle quite easily, assuming that everyone uses the same form of storage, such as magnetic tape.

BESSINGER   How many channels?

VENEZKY   That brings up another problem which I mentioned in the report we are discussing.

SMITH   How serious is this? There are IBM installations with seven-channel tapes and nine-channel tapes. There again it's cost but I don't know that it's very great.

VENEZKY   The cost is not very serious. We are talking about a copy of a 2,400 foot tape, probably at about $50 or less. It should be much cheaper once more installations have conversion equipment.

SMITH   I would think a multi-program environment would be cheaper. What do you think?

ROBERSON I agree. I'd like to make one point. I'm not sure I'd agree with the data preparation. It may be as naïve as we just discussed. If a person is using an upper and lower case keypunch, as opposed to a standard 029, then your considerations, in terms of programming, change as well. This is not just a question of coding, it's a question of different characters in the keypunch directly acceptable by the computer. And if your programs are written to, say, look for slash to indicate capital letters as opposed to having capital letters actually punched, it's a completely different matter.

VENEZKY Well, there is really little you can do about that. If people are going to use the full eight-bit code, there is no simple way to make these compatible with six-bit codes other than to translate six-bit codes to eight-bit codes. That means you don't have the same materials encoded, upper and lower case, unless some linear scheme like that I have proposed is adopted. Then you need a program to convert from end-of-word coding to in-place coding. How many installations are we talking about, though, that are concerned with upper and lower case, separately identified on the keyboard?

ROBERSON We use upper and lower case.

VENEZKY How many others do who are here now? One solution is to normalize on a six-bit lower case code.

ROBERSON You would convert to that?

VENEZKY No, I would stay with that and let those people who use upper- and lower-case codes convert to it.

ROBERSON That sounds like regression. I should think it would be interesting putting our data in the same format as the manuscript, and not regressing to the requirements of the machine.

VENEZKY That's not what I am saying. You will do whatever is best for your own interest. To distribute this, given that the majority of the centres do not handle eight-bit code, we would have to reduce it to six-bit code somehow. The easiest thing to do is actually write a little program that in the process of conversion will retain linear sequence information that you have by separate codes. That is, add characters at the end or somewhere. Do you see what I mean? We have no choice, given that the majority of installations use six-channel tapes.

F. ROBINSON I would like to ask a simple question to bring us back to the general context of the dictionary. When you talk about standardizing and merging and so on, are you looking toward the ultimate conflation of a large number of independent concordances into one massive Old English concordance? Well, there is no prospect, is there, of a retrospective conflation? Pillsbury, Venezky, and Bessinger seem to contain different *amounts* of information, different *kinds* of information, and so on. These could never be conflated into a single concordance, could they?

VENEZKY With a little preprocessing.

F. ROBINSON As of now, you could take them up where they are and put them together by reducing them to a sort of lowest common denomination of information, or something like that?

BESSINGER   It's not practical.

SMITH   One of the things that has bothered me about the discussion of conflating concordances is that our concordance doesn't exist. This thing which is printed doesn't exist in machine form any more. It does *not* exist.

BESSINGER   The *tapes* exist.

SMITH   Not of the concordance. Maybe of the six-volume concordance, but not of *Beowulf.* Nothing exists of *Beowulf* except the text. I believe that is true. It never occured to me to save this final product. It's a shock. I always assumed my problem was to get the programs going so that I could generate the final product from scratch and I did it umpteen times until I got it right, or as right as it is. It never occured to me to do anything but worry about the program! I think it is because I lived inside IBM and machine time was plentiful, but maybe there are other people in this situation.

BESSINGER   You see the general point is that all of us are throwing away money like drunken sailors.

SMITH   Other people's money.

BESSINGER   Yes! And we must start thinking about collaboration and correlation of effort before this goes too much farther. I still don't know what you mean by not having any machine form of *Beowulf.* We have three separate tapes, do we not, which contain the *Beowulf* concorded and unconcorded along with the rest of Krapp-Dobbie?

SMITH   Yes.

BESSINGER   One of them is up in Waterloo. I brought it up yesterday.

SMITH   Well, good. I hope it's better than I think.

BESSINGER   It's one with hyphens and homograph indicators.

SMITH   May I also ask a question of those who have had experience in making compatible versions of various different keypunched texts (I am not talking about concordances for a minute, just talking about texts). How difficult do you think this is? I personally am of two minds. The National Science Foundation sponsored an investigation a few years ago of the feasibility, nothing more, of a national centre for texts in machine-readable form, and some very bright guys at Ramo-Wooldridge, people that I respect highly, looked into this. They came up with the conclusion that in order to use another man's text the cost of writing programs to convert his text to your format is so great, that the break-even point was 900,000 words of text; in other words, for less than 900,000 words you might as well rekeypunch. Now, at the time, I didn't quite agree with the way they came to this conclusion. They took the cost of the Sage project in dollars per ultimate instruction, when the whole thing was done, and figured how many machine instructions would be needed to convert a text from one form to another and then multiplied it out and got this fantastic cost and compared it with the keypunch. I didn't agree with that. It all seemed terribly simple to me and yet I may be very wrong. You must, Professor Venezky, have had experience which makes you bring this up.

VENEZKY   Well, my experience has been that it doesn't take too much processing to use the Old English texts that I have obtained from other persons. That is, it did not take an experienced programmer very long to convert them to a form that I was able to manipulate. I found it irritating, though, that the most trivial, arbitrary decisions caused the amount of trouble that they did. For example, when two characters were used for a single symbol rather than one. If there had been substitutional co-operation initially, a lot of money would have been saved; maybe we shouldn't make an issue of all this. What happens if we try to make distributable just the input text? I am beginning to feel the more we talk about this that the Old English materials centre should obtain the input texts and rerun concordances under one concordance program to guarantee that when all concordances are run we can merge them without trouble. Now this guarantees that the maximum duplication is 100 per cent. It may in reality turn out to be less. But certainly not 500 per cent, not 1,000 per cent, as is possible now. Maybe another approach is to encourage people not to run concordances on their own, but to prepare the data in the format that a particular concordance programmer will accept, assuming that we all agree on what is a good way to run a concordance. Then have them send the tape and a blank cheque or whatever else the financial arrangements may require to the centre. This organization would then generate a concordance and send one copy to the originator and keep another copy for themselves. Maybe that is a more practical approach.

BESSINGER   The circulation of ad hoc concordances is certainly going to be a feature, I think, of the near future. Small concordances, special concordances, which are made with relatively limited materials and used for relatively limited purposes, but which you don't want to throw away when you're through – one might be willing to circulate these in some pretty rough or sketchy format, which wouldn't be suitable for formal publication; it wouldn't be needed.

VENEZKY   I would like to make an offer to people here and to anyone you would like to carry this offer to. If you will prepare materials for concordances in the format for our concordance program, and send us either the sheets written out for keypunching or the cards with the card images on tape, we will run, free of charge, the concordance and send you back a copy. I am doing this for several reasons. I am interested in it as an experiment – and let me qualify this offer by saying I will process a reasonable amount of material and I don't know what the reasonable is, but will arrive at it somehow. It also gives me material in a hurry that I might want to use for my studies and, finally, I would like to show people that it is possible to do concordances without gaining 50 per cent more grey hair. I sense from the comments here that there is still a credibility gap.

PILLSBURY   I think one thing we might take into consideration is the matter of transliteration if we are not thinking about a printout text which has upper and lower, æ,þ, ð, and the rest. I think this is the situation for quite a while longer. So far we haven't considered the readers very much, and while linguists are capable of reading dollar signs as þ's and asterisks as æ's and all kinds of things, I think you will find an immediate resistance on the part of the old-line philologists and the non-linguistically trained readers who cannot read dollar signs with quite as much facility as linguists can. The old-line humanists expect upper and lower case þ and æ and so forth. Obviously, for some time we are not going to be able to duplicate those, but I think we do get into an aesthetic problem about approximating or suggesting as closely as we can the shape of the idiosyncratic Old English graphs with whatever manipulation we use.

VENEZKY   There are several views on this particular problem. The selection of symbols to substitute, given that we have no choice – that we can only produce what the printer will print – this selection can be based upon either perceptual considerations, that is, making the keypunch symbols look as much like the Old English graph as possible, or upon considerations of cost. Punching an upper-case symbol takes more time and consequently more money than punching a lower-case symbol. Don't confuse this with upper- and lower-case alphabetics. One arrives at the numbers and some of the special symbols on a keypunch by shifting to upper case. You still have a limited set of symbols.

   If you are doing a very large concordance the number of characters that require upper-case shifts can add an appreciable cost to the keypunching procedure and therefore to the cost of the entire concordance. So there are really two views on this. I personally have not found very much resistance, as long as there aren't a large number of symbols, to almost any set of symbol substitutions. Now, perhaps people here have had other experiences. One way to look at this is to say we are not going to get tomorrow's jobs with yesterday's skills, or perhaps we are all going to have to learn to recognize on a page that asterisk stands for æ and a plus sign for ð, a dollar sign for þ or whatever. I think that we can all do that.

BESSINGER   I can say that Dr Smith was very generous in preparing interim concordances, ad hoc lists of various kinds, for me in the preparation of our book. We ran several control experiments, laboratory experiments, as it were, on the proofreading of different compatible and incompatible types, that is, types incompatible to human beings. When a þ was 6 and ð was 7 we got these concordances at sixes and sevens, and we were trying to proofread our text this way. The percentage of human error in the proofreading skyrocketed, though of course, one could remember from line to line that a 6 was a þ and a ð was 7. It just distracted you from looking for other things that as an editor you might be wanting to correct, or to question, and so on. It's putting a degree of linguistic noise into the program that will have to be filtered out before any very severe proof-reading can be done. I agree that, for certain limited purposes and temporary uses, almost any kind of graph system would be acceptable to most of us here. We are not talking about going permanently into print.

VENEZKY   We print out, actually the computer prints out, at the bottom of every page in our concordance, if we put in the information, the symbol used and then the name of it – so if one symbol is forgotten, just scan to the bottom and the symbol substitution is on every page.

BESSINGER   But it's not that you forget; it's that it adds this noise, this irritant, to the linguistic communication on the page which is another level of information that the editor's mind has to cope with.

VENEZKY   I don't think that there is any solution to that if we do want to distribute ad hoc concordances.

BESSINGER   Yes, as long as we are doing that ...

VENEZKY   I am not advocating that for publishing. What do you recommend for how we should proceed from here? Should there be a committee set up which then arrives at a series of standards and distributes these for comments within a set period of time? Do you think that would be better than continuing this discussion?

CAMERON   Well, at least we have made a start. Now we want a chance to look at these proposals.

LEYERLE   I wonder if I might, at this point, talk about some tendencies which I note from our discussion; this is meant as a generalized summary which we might discuss individually over lunch, reserving part of the session this afternoon to reach the kind of conclusions that you were just suggesting, Professor Venezky. I noted down eight points, three from the first session and five from the second.

First, I felt that there was a tendency among the people speaking to support the need for a centre, at some unspecified location, oriented toward research in the humanities by use of computer technology.

The second was that our work should be mutually compatible and that the programs, such as they are developing, should be – I think the word was – converging; I am a little hesitant here because I am ignorant of computers.

The third tendency was that there should be an anticipation of the needs which this material might be required to serve; in setting up the programs and in deciding the way in which the material is being presented, a good deal of hard thinking should go into what kind of questions would be asked of it.

At the session this morning I noted five more points. Again just tendencies.

The first, that concordances by use of computers are obviously well underway and that the technology, although difficult, is capable of solution; I am impressed by the speed and vigour with which the work is being done, and also by the extraordinarily informative – to me, at least – accounts that we heard this morning. I would hope that we would get some information on similar programs outside North America. Perhaps this silence is significant; perhaps this is where the work is being done. If this is true, it seems to me also a significant tendency.

The second point is that, despite problems of a technical nature, concordances can be prepared by computers with the capability of giving much more information than would be otherwise obtainable except through the most laborious hand compilation.

The third point is that there exists considerable experimentation in the method by which these concordances are being put together, ranging all the way from computing an edition, as the Bessinger-Smith concordance to *Beowulf* – now happily out – to Walter Bak's interest in computing directly from the manuscripts. This range gives us the parameters; within these we should consider where we would focus.

My next point is the possibility (which is to me intriguing), put forward by Professor Venezky, that the output for distribution be put in machine-readable form. We heard about the enormous space needed to store cards, and the printouts themselves are, of course, very large; the idea of having magnetic tapes which could be used and circulated easily is a very interesting idea which would solve daunting technical problems.

Finally, my last point. There should be – and this reverts to my first point – a materials centre where such procedures might be standardized and focused.

I don't know whether you'd all agree with these tendencies and I don't really mean them to be anything more than my own impressions of the discussions thus far; I hope we can draw together similar tendencies in our session this afternoon about dictionaries, primarily because our hope for this conference is to develop these sorts of tendencies from which we can reach conclusions which we would all support.

CONCORDANCES AND DICTIONARIES

LEYERLE   There is a slight alteration in the order of speakers. Bruce Mitchell will be starting, followed by Christopher Ball; otherwise it is as your program. I think that, talking with you individually, I have the impression that you would like us to move on from computers and individual problems which computers have presented, directly to the problem of the dictionary or dictionaries, and then finally to a session at the end in which we would have a general discussion of principles and departures so that we know in a sense what we would like to do, if we can agree on it. I would ask you to reflect a bit about what proposals you would wish to make about committees or directions or schemes that we could agree to before we break up. I think I speak for the meeting that, as I can sense it, many of us feel it would be a pity if we stopped short of formulating what it is that we would like to see happen. I would like, then, without further ado, to ask Bruce Mitchell to talk to you. He will be reporting on a meeting which took place a week ago today in London.

MITCHELL   Professor Leyerle, ladies and gentlemen. 'It is good for us to be here,' one of the Disciples once said on a mountain. I feel that today, and I thank the Centre for Medieval Studies and the University of Toronto for providing the opportunity, and for what I, as an Australian, would like to describe as their 'Colonially lavish hospitality.' (That is meant as a compliment!) It is good for us to be here greeting old friends and meeting in the flesh scholars who up to now have been only books, articles, or, dare I mouth it, footnotes. It is good for us to be here initiating the transmogrification of Bosworth-Toller's *Anglo-Saxon Dictionary*, Professor Alistair Campbell's new supplement for which is now at the press. It is good for us to be here remembering that the transmogrification of Bosworth-Toller's *Anglo-Saxon Dictionary* is not a process which will take place overnight. The present position of the *Middle English Dictionary*, I am sure you will agree, and of the supplement to the *Oxford English Dictionary* reminds us all too clearly that the making of dictionaries is a slow business. Haste is not of the essence. Some of you here today may live to handle the new Old English dictionary which we all see as one of our ultimate aims. I doubt if I will, even though my insurance company still seems to think that I am a pretty good risk. But I'd like to voice a fear which I have now, and that is my fear that, if the complete comprehensiveness of concordances outlined today is insisted on, the more limited objective of the Dictionary will be even further postponed.

Today I bring what are known in English Trade Union circles as 'fraternal greetings' from the Anglo-Saxon scholars of the United Kingdom and of Europe. My accent may lead you to think that my qualifications for this task are dubious, but I recently had the privilege of being elected secretary of the European editorial committee set up to share in the project for a new Old English dictionary. My present task is to explain briefly what we have done and to make several points on behalf of the committee. Four of its members are present here today: Peter Clemoes, Elrington and Bosworth professor-elect of Anglo-Saxon at Cambridge; James Cross, professor of English language at Liverpool; Eric Stanley, professor of English language at Queen Mary College, London; and Christopher Ball, fellow of Lincoln College, Oxford. Their presence gives me a confidence I should otherwise lack. I bring apologies and best wishes from Professor Alistair Campbell of Oxford and Professor Helmut Gneuss of Munich.

First, then, a brief history of what we have done. When Professor Stanley Kahrl returned from the meeting of Group I Officers of the MLA in New York in October, he wrote to Professor Norman Davis. As a result, Professor Davis, Professor Alistair Campbell, and myself met Professor Kahrl at Oxford on 22 November 1968. Our discussion there and our subsequent actions have all been based on the proposals reported to us by Professor Kahrl, now set out in paragraph 2 of the report of the meeting of the Group I Officers in New York on 15 and 16 October 1968. Now I speak of the situation as we understood it and this proposal, as we understood, envisaged what might be called the dictionary committee, whose task it would be to exercise general supervision over the project. We have found that Professor Alistair Campbell and Professor Helmut Gneuss were willing to serve on this committee and, as we understood it, a North American representative is to be appointed. Now, again as we understood it, under this committee there were to operate two sub-committees – the computer committee with Professor Bessinger as chairman, and the editorial committee, and I quote here what I understood the latter's task would be; I am quoting from the motion approved at the October meeting, which states the function of the Editorial Committee in these words: 'To determine what Old English prose texts need to be edited or re-edited, and keep up with the editing that is under way. The Committee could publish lists of desiderata, suggest specifications for good editing, and perhaps confer seals of approval upon new editions which it feels are adequate for use in preparing concordances for dictionaries.' From what we read of the minutes of the special meeting called in December 1968, this motion was confirmed at that special meeting. I believe also that this committee was to operate in both North America and Europe, and Professor Kahrl reported to us in Oxford that Professor Collins, Professor Irving, and Professor Rosier had agreed to head the North American Committee, initially.

The task which we undertook as the result of our meeting with Professor Kahrl in November was the establishment of what I call, for convenience, the European editorial committee, to carry out the functions approved by the October meeting of Group I, those functions I have just quoted. On this basis the committee has now been established and we have been fortunate in finding these scholars willing to serve: Alistair Campbell, Helmut Gneuss, Peter Clemoes, James Cross, Eric Stanley, and Christopher Ball.

I am acting at the moment as secretary, and we are to issue an invitation to Professor R. Derolez of the University of Ghent to join us. That, as I have said, was the organization which we understood was envisaged as the possibility by the MLA meeting and it is of course an organization which is capable of modification in any way which might seem acceptable to this meeting. However, we do see these three broad divisions as important. Obviously there is a computer committee and it will come as no surprise to anybody, I suppose, if I suggest that knowledge of computer techniques applied to Old English is truly far more advanced in North America than it is in Europe. Secondly, we would see an editorial committee responsible for the nature of the materials to be fed into the concordances and so into the dictionary. In a moment I shall be reporting on what the European committee felt last week, but I do know that later on Dr Peter Clemoes from Cambridge wishes to say something from the floor about the concept of the manuscript as something unchanging. Thirdly, of course, we see the need for a dictionary committee which is, as we see it, to be responsible for deciding what the dictionary is to contain. I am not going to say anything more about that at the moment because Mr Ball's paper deals with some aspects of this problem.

I turn now to what happened when the full European Editorial Committee met last Saturday, 15 March, in University College, London, with Professor Campbell in the chair. There were several minor matters discussed which I won't bother to mention. The secretary was authorized to appeal at a later stage for grants-in-aid to bodies such as the British Academy and the Leverhulme Trust, but of course such appeals must wait until we have something firm which, as Professor Leyerle said, we hope will emerge from today's meeting. The committee then heard a full report from Professor Kahrl on the special meeting of Group I in December 1968, and on the reasons for the convening of this present conference, and it had before it the informal minutes of the December meeting of Group I, set out in volume II, number 2 of the *Old English Newsletter* of February 1969. As a result of what we were told and as a result of what we read in those minutes, we conducted a discussion concerning general principles and procedures, and in particular a discussion about the question which we gathered it was one of the main objects of this present conference to debate: whether the computer concordances, and hence the new Old English dictionary, should be compiled from existing editions, when suitable, and from editions to be commissioned, or from manuscripts or the facsimiles of manuscripts. During this discussion the following points, among others, were made. Firstly, the possibility of providing printed texts of unpublished material, such as homilies; secondly, the heavy responsibility which would be placed on a keypuncher editor; thirdly, what we saw as the difficulty of checking a keypuncher's work without an intermediate printed stage and the resulting possibility of the introduction of non-words; and fourthly, the importance of references to standard editions for the convenience of users of the dictionary. If subsequently a new edition became standard, marginal references could be given to the edition used in the compilation of the dictionary, as Miller's edition of Bede's *Ecclesiastical History*[1] gives references to Smith's edition[2] still valuable for the syntactician and as Dr Clemoes' forthcoming edition of Aelfric's Homilies is to give references to Thorpe.[3] Doubtless all these points have already been made in debate over here, and (I have just had to write in a footnote) some of them have indeed been made today. But I hope you will agree that I should mention them, as they were part of our deliberations.

Now, at the conclusion of this discussion I, as secretary, was instructed to record the following: firstly, that this meeting was most grateful to Professor Kahrl for his report; secondly, that the meeting, while interested in the proposal that the concordances and hence the dictionary should be prepared direct from manuscripts or facsimiles instead of from edited texts, was deeply concerned about the resulting loss, and here I quote Professor Campbell, 'of so many sound and sometimes excellent scholarly editions'; thirdly, that the meeting, while agreeing that archaic editions like Spelman's *Psalter* should be dropped, wondered whether it was wise to abandon satisfactory or good existing editions in favour of manuscripts. Indeed, as a voice not represented here today was heard to say, 'Would it not be a reckless procedure not to use to the full Professor Pope's *Aelfric*?' Fourthly, that the meeting urged the necessity for making new texts of unedited or badly edited works; these could be transcripts with a minimal amount of editing or full new editions, depending on the circumstance. Facsimiles and microfilms of manuscripts would be of great service in correcting the existing printed texts. Finally, that the meeting was strongly in favour of the scheme propounded in October and set out in the minutes of the meeting of Group I Officers in New York on 15 and 16 October, that is to say the establishment of editorial committees in particular with the functions which I quoted previously. To adopt any other scheme, the meeting felt, would be to cast away the editorial work of past and present scholars. I think this is also the view of Professor Norman Davis.

Well, this then, Mr Chairman, ladies and gentlemen, was the feeling of the European editorial committee which met in London last Saturday. As I have

1   Thomas Miller, *The Old English Version of Bede's Ecclesiastical History of the English People* Early English Text Society, o.s. 95, 96, 110, 111 (London, 1890-99); reprinted for the Society by Oxford University Press, London, 1959 (part I, text and translation) and 1963 (part II, collation of the MSS).

2   John Smith, ed., *Ecclesiasticae historiae gentis anglorum, libri quinque* (Cambridge, 1722).

3   Benjamin Thorpe, ed., *The Homilies of the Anglo-Saxon Church, the First Part, Containing the Sermones Catholici or Homilies of Aelfric*, 2 vols. (London, 1844-46).

already said, four of its members are present here today and I know that some of them wish to supplement what I have said.

The time is coming near for me to conclude this report and, as I come into the straight and approach the finishing line, I am tempted to desert my present sober steed for that best-of-all hobby horses, Old English syntax. The thought of a beautiful array of computer concordances listing all the Old English conjunctions and of rows of computers waiting to print them out in their context raises me in my imagination to a state of syntactical ecstasy in which I could float for a long time. But such states of ecstasy are difficult to achieve in reality. Keyword in context references to conjunctions like 'þeah' and 'þenden' will, I should imagine, provide the syntactician with all he needs about them. There are other problems not so amenable. The obvious example that occurs to me is that splendid Old English maid-of-all-work 'þa,' the accusative singular feminine and nominative accusative plural of all genders of both demonstrative and relative (frequently indistinguishable because we lack the vital clue of intonation) and also an adverb and conjunction (again often indistinguishable for the same reason). The pronoun and conjunction 'þæt' is another example. To what extent is the syntactician justified in expecting the computer to sort out these functions? Can he expect to say to the computer: 'Pick out all the examples of "þa" conjunction or adverb as against "þa" pronoun'? (It is, I should say, impossible for us to expect it to distinguish 'þa' adverb from 'þa' conjunction since I know of no criteria by which I can distinguish them in situations of real ambiguity.) At what stage is the computer to be asked to make these distinctions – the distinctions which can be made? Will they be made from keyword-in-context printouts or are these distinctions to be signalled as the text is punched? If the latter, will the syntactician have already spent on the task any time which the computer might have saved him? These are some of the difficulties which I see for the syntactician who seeks to use the computer to get the raw material on which to exercise his mind. Well, as I say, I am asking these questions which exercise my mind. I see my life slipping by. Can I wait for the computer?

But it is time now, Mr Chairman, for me to sit down. Before doing so I should like to stress that there is in the United Kingdom and on the continent of Europe considerable enthusiasm for the production of a new Old English dictionary. It has certainly become clear from informal conversations that there will be no difficulty in finding a publisher for a new Old English dictionary if the project comes to fruition. As I write this in Oxford (I have down here), I am confident that, as a result of the combined wisdom of this conference, the dictionary will ultimately be delivered safely. There was recently a report in an English newspaper that a computer at the Royal Air Force Record Centre had discharged an airman because he was pregnant. Soon, no doubt, a computer will be carrying the yet-to-be-born Old English dictionary. And to that infant dictionary I say 'Good Luck, dear book ... "Wes þu hal, boc leofe."'

LEYERLE   Thank you very much indeed. I wonder, Professor Clemoes, if this might be the time for you to add your remarks.

CLEMOES   Thank you for this opportunity. I think Dr Mitchell has identified three areas in each of which expert knowledge has got to contribute to a dictionary. One very obviously is the technology of the computer. Another is, of course, an understanding of the dictionary itself: what the dictionary itself shall comprise. The third area is the one I want to make a remark about: that is, the expert knowledge required in preparing the material to be fed into the computer. Mr Bak has clearly grappled with the problem of how to convert manuscript texts into computer material. In the account he gave us this morning, he referred to what he sees as the nature of manuscript evidence – that it supplies a constant standard: the manuscript existed 1,000 years ago, it exists today, and it will exist tomorrow, unchanging. This of course is true of it as a physical object. But what I'd like to stress is that as soon as a manuscript is used for any purpose whatever, an inconstant element immediately enters; any use of a manuscript is, I would claim, essentially an essay in interpretation; and I think that so far as relating this to the dictionary project is concerned, one must ask very carefully what the processes of interpretation are.

I think a manuscript as raw material for conversion into computer material requires interpretation because of two main kinds of characteristics that it has. One is that it supplies only partial evidence, if one takes into account things like punctuation or word division which were mentioned this morning. The scribe writing a manuscript did not have the distinctions clearly in mind that we need to apply in using this material today. He didn't have a clear view of the presence, or absence, of word division as being the kind of distinction of which we are conscious today. Very often there will be such a shading off that one will not honestly be able to say whether there is word division at a particular point in a manuscript or not; and this sort of indefiniteness applies over the whole range of the evidence. For instance, capitals: the same gradation is present. Some letters are clearly capitals; some are clearly not; but then there is a large category which is neither one thing nor the other. Or, if you like, punctuation: the punctuation in the manuscripts leaves untouched a great many functions that we attribute to punctuation today. And not only that: complications enter into it. Punctuation is not a stable thing: users of the manuscript tend to tamper with it, change it – by erasure or by additions. All this makes the use of the evidence supplied by the manuscripts extremely complicated.

This sort of complexity is the second problem which I think manuscript material poses. One, as I have said, is the partial evidence it offers on many things that are important to us, the other is the complexity of it. I think there are two main sources of complexity – or kinds of complexity. One is that the manuscript is a self-contained homogeneous unit. And, if you like, the state of affairs with regard to punctuation offers an illustration of this. Within the limits of a manuscript's evidence, its features are inter-related, so that the interpretation of punctuation is related to the interpre-tation of, let us say, capitals and spacing. And one can come to a sound judgment on this kind of question only by study of the manuscript itself. I don't think it is possible from a photograph: from a photograph one simply cannot estimate the balance which these interrelated factors have. That's one kind of complexity, I would say, which is essentially one of interpretation. The other one is that the interpretation of one manuscript depends on knowledge of the other existing manuscripts – if one has, say, four or five copies of a single text. Let us suppose that the scribe has omitted a line from his exemplar: there is obviously a need to make good the sense. All right, someone has made it good. Has he made it good auth-entically, from a knowledge of another copy, or has he made it good out of his own head? This simply cannot be determined without a knowledge of what is in the other manuscripts. This, then, is another form of com-plexity that one comes up against in dealing with manuscripts: not only does one need to have a sense of a manuscript as an interrelated unit in its own right, but one also has to have as much sense of it as one can acquire in relation to other existing manuscripts of the same text.

LEYERLE Thank you very much, Professor Clemoes. I wonder if before we discuss the report of Dr Mitchell and Professor Clemoes' remarks, we might hear from Mr Ball, who will also be representing, I think, the view emanating from this committee meeting a week ago.

BALL Mr Chairman, I should not allow your last remark; I think my remarks are entirely personal and I hope my colleagues won't oppose them too strenu-ously. It would be unfair to saddle them with them. I should like, before I start, to thank you and your colleagues for the magnificent hospitality with which you have entertained us. I feel it as a great honour that I have been invited to speak at this conference, since I know but little about dictionaries and still less about computers (though I have been learning fast in the last twenty-four hours). What I want to do is to lay before you some thoughts about dictionary-making and, in particular, the problems of making an Old English dictionary.

I start with the proposition that it would be rash to proceed with a pro-gram of computer concordances until one had first decided (in broad out-line) what kind of a dictionary was planned and what sorts of information it should contain. It might well prove to be the case that the details of the computer concordance program would vary, depending on the type of dic-tionary that it was ultimately hoped to produce. It would be little short of disastrous if, after the expensive mechanical part of the work was completed, the editors of the dictionary were to discover that they were being provided with the wrong sort of information, or information which was incomplete in some important respects.

What sort of a dictionary, then, do we want for Old English? This may seem a silly question; dictionary-making reached a state of near-perfection in the nineteenth century, and twentieth-century linguists have made relatively few important new contributions to the theory of lexicography. It is our habit (at least, it is our habit in Oxford), to point to the *Oxford English Dictionary* as an ideal. But I would wish to insert two caveats here: (i) that we should not overlook some recent work on lexicology which suggests new approaches in dictionary-making; and (ii) that we should recognize the special problems that Old English presents to the lexicographer.

Let me consider these special problems first. I would particularly stress the following three factors:
the paucity of the material;
the uncertainty of the date of many of the texts, which makes it difficult to plan a dictionary on strict historical principles; and
the fact that most of the material consists of direct or indirect glosses of Latin texts.
There is little that we can do about the paucity of the material: but this factor does raise the question of the importance to Old English lexicography of evidence from the other Germanic languages, and (more importantly) from Middle English and even New English. I am not here arguing that the dictionary should (or should not) have an etymological element: this is a separate issue, though it is one which we shall have to discuss in due course. What I am suggesting is that in some cases our knowledge of the meaning of words in Old English depends not a little on the evidence of other Germanic languages and of Middle English and New English. We shall have to decide how far, and according to what principles, such evidence is to be admitted into the dictionary.

The question of whether the dictionary should be planned on historical principles is another difficult problem which should (I think) be resolved before too much work is undertaken. But I merely wish to state the problems now and immediately pass on to the more complex difficulty of the place of Latin in Old English lexicography.

Clearly much of the most crucial evidence for the meaning of Old English words is the Latin texts which are glossed or translated into Old English. In the case of interlinear glosses it is obvious that the Latin word and context is usually more important than the Old English context for the determination of the sense of the Old English word. One hopes that any computer concordance program would take this into account, and that the relevant context of the word would include both the Old English and the Latin. In the case of continuous texts which are more or less directly translated from Latin, again the Latin source would seem indispensible to the lexicographer, and it would obviously be convenient if the computer could present him with parallel texts. As one proceeds to the Old English texts which, though based on Latin works, are in no way close translations, the usefulness of the Latin source (or sources) to the lexicographer recedes. Where to draw the line is the problem. And this problem seems to me to be a glaring example of the kind of editorial decision which must be taken before the program of the computer concordances can get under way.

I wish now to turn to some recent work on lexicology which, I suggest, we might want to take into account before deciding what kind of a dictionary to produce. I am aware of three new departures in this field: others present may be able to add more. First, the work of Professor Chomsky and his associates has recently made much of the concept of the *lexicon* as a store for much detailed grammatical information. We shall have to decide what sort of grammatical labelling we wish to put in the dictionary, and how detailed we wish or are able to make this information. Secondly, the neo-Firthian linguists of Edinburgh (mainly connected with Professor Angus McIntosh) have been developing the concept of *collocation* to describe such lexical patterns as a 'powerful car' (but not a 'strong car'), 'strong tea' (but not 'powerful tea'), beside both a 'strong argument' and a 'powerful argument.' The Firth memorial volume edited by C. E. Bazell[4] and others contains important articles on this subject by Professors Halliday and Sinclair, together with an interesting attempt to apply it to Old English by Miss Marjorie Daunt. Thirdly, I would draw your attention to Professor John Lyons' recent work on *meaning,* and in particular to his suggestion that meaning should be stated, wherever possible, in terms of the four sense-relationships of *identity, inclusion, incompatibility,* and *opposition.*[5] A semantic analysis of this sort could well be made within the framework of a dictionary. I do not claim that any new Old English dictionary must follow novel lines or bow to the prevailing lexicographical fashions, but I think we should carefully consider these new proposals before rejecting them.

As an example of the kind of information we might try to incorporate in a new dictionary I have laid before you some examples drawn from a glossary to Cædmon's *Hymn,* Bede's *Deathsong* and the *Leiden Riddle* on which I am working at present (see appendix, pp. 93-4). The information given is laid out in seven sections, as follows:

1 grammatical information
2 derivational information
3 the lexical sub-language to which the word belongs (if any)
4 relevant citations

4 C. E. Bazell, J. C. Catford, M. A. K. Halliday, R. H. Robins, eds., *In Memory of J. R. Firth* (London, 1966).

5 J. Lyons, *Structural Semantics* (Oxford, 1963), *Introduction to Theoretical Linguistics* (Cambridge, 1968).

5 synonyms, antonyms, and hyponyms
6 the corresponding word in the Latin translations of these poems (if any),
   and the appropriate New English translation
7 the relevant headword in Bosworth-Toller and the main senses of the word

For grammar-words (cf. 'aefter') there is an abbreviated form of entry.
This is, of course, by no means an exhaustive list of the types of lexical
information one might give; I have intentionally omitted, for instance,
etymologies and evidence from Middle English and New English. The principle behind this glossary is that the reader should be given, as far as possible,
all the relevant information about a word which a native speaker of Old
English might have had.

I would draw your attention to some particular points: first, the in-
adequate nature of the grammatical labelling. It is our tradition to state the
morphological details of a word with considerable precision but more or
less to disregard any syntactic restrictions that may apply to it. In an ideal
dictionary I should like to see *adjectives,* for instance, labelled as comparable or incomparable (e.g. New English 'male,' 'left,' etc.), predicative or
non-predicative (e.g. 'only,' 'other,' etc) prenominal or postnominal (e.g.
'concerned' in one of its senses), and so on. Some of these syntactic categories apply to Old English directly, for example, comparability of adjectives.
But there are many other applicable to the four major word-classes, and it
is my view that this sort of information can be (and should be) stated in an
ideal dictionary. But, of course, we shall have to wait to see Dr Mitchell's
projected syntax before we can go very far in this direction.

Secondly, I would urge you to consider the establishment of lexical sub-
languages. I have tried to operate with five categories: poetic, religious,
dialect, foreign, and rare; the last-named is merely a label to indicate that
all known citations for the word are listed (e.g. 'deothdaege'). I would hope
that the projected dictionary could attempt something far subtler, distin-
guishing words by dialect, date, genre, and so on. One would like to see the
vocabulary sifted according to a variety of criteria: prose *versus* verse has
already been done, but religious *versus* secular, translated literature *versus*
non-translated texts, might produce interesting, interlocking varieties of
lexical sub-languages.

Thirdly, I would draw your attention to the sketchy attempt to state the
sense-relations of Old English words in terms of synonymy (= sign), an-
tonymy (≠ sign), and hyponymy (or inclusion of sense: ⊂ sign). This, if
done carefully, could, I think, add considerably to the value of an Old
English dictionary, but one must guard against the danger of imposing the
sense-relations of New English words on the Old English material.

The following extracts from a glossary are not presented in order to lay
down any definite program for a dictionary. Far from it. My own ideas on
the subject are still only partly formed and I am sure others will not agree
with all the things that I have suggested might be included, and will be able

to think of things that I have omitted. My point is a simple one. We must not fall into the habit of thinking that writing a dictionary entry is a straightforward matter or that we all know and agree what material should be in a dictionary. Before any program of computer concordances can get under way we must (I suggest) decide in principle what the new dictionary is to be like, and lay down guidelines for the concordance projects. Professor Bessinger said yesterday 'Computers do not reduce a scholar's relevant work.' I suggest that our most pressing and most relevant work is to establish a group of lexicographers who will first have the task of planning the contents of the dictionary and instructing those responsible for the concordances as to the sorts of information the dictionary-makers will require.

APPENDIX: EXTRACTS FROM A GLOSSARY
Cædmon's *Hymn* (CH), Bede's *Deathsong* (BDS), *The Leiden Riddle* (LR)
All line references are to texts in *The Anglo-Saxon Poetic Records*.

allmectig adj., *a/ō*-stem, CH9 nom. sg. masc. (strong)
eall (*eallhalig*, etc.); *mihtig* (*felamihtig*, etc.):
miht (cf. **maecti**); *-ig* (**halig**, **freorig**, etc.); *eallmiht*.
religious
frea ælmihtig Genesis 5,116, *Judith* 300, *Christ* 1378,
Paris Psalter 85.17, etc. (cf. *god æ., meotud æ.,*
cyning æ., drihten æ., etc.)
= *eallcræftig, eallwealdende;* ⊂ *mihtig*
'*omnipotens*, almighty'
(*ælmihtig*, 'almighty')

aefter prep. (with dat.) BDS5 '*post*, after'
adv. (**æfter**) CH8 '*dehinc*, afterwards'

aelda n. masc. *i*-stem (only pl.) CH5 gen.
eald
poetic
ælda bearnum Christ 936, *ylda bearnum Genesis* 2472,
Daniel 106, *Beowulf* 150, etc.
= *menn*, **firas**, *guman*, **hæleþ**(*as*), *leode, niþþas.*
'*homines*, men'
(*ilde*, 'men, mankind')

brogum n. masc. *n*-stem, LR13 dat. pl.
herebroga, etc.; *bregan*
—
Oft þær broga cwom / egeslic ond uncuð Guthlac 140
(cf. *Paris Psalter* 87.16, 103.8, *Guthlac* 84, *Riddle* 3.51)
= **egsa**, *ege, fyrhtu, gryre*
'terror'
(*brōga*, 'monster, danger, terror, dread')

deothdaege   n. masc. *a*-stem, BDS5 dat. sg.

deaþ (*deaþbedd*, etc.); *dead*; *dæg* (*feorhdæg*, etc.).
poetic, rare
*wel biδ þæm þe mot / æfter deaδdæge drihten secean
Beowulf* 187, *Sigemunde gesprong / æfter deaδdæge
dom unlytel Beowulf* 885, *Meotod ana wat / hwyder seo
sawul sceal syδδan hweorfan, / and ealle þa gastas
þe for gode hweorfaδ/æfter deaδdæge, domes bidaδ /
on fæder fæδme Maxims* II,60, *þæt me þuhte ful oft
þæt hit wær(e) XXX þusend wintra / to þinum deaδdæge
Soul and Body* I,37
⊂ *dæg*
'(*exitus*), death-day'
(*deaþdæg*, 'death-day')

egsan   n. masc. *n*-stem, LR13 gen. sg.

egeslic, etc.; *flodegesa*, etc.; *egesian*, *egesung*; *ege*
–

*ær him fær godes / þurh egesan gryre aldre
gesceode Daniel* 592 (cf. *Daniel* 466, *Christ and
Satan* 452, 725)
broga, *ege, fyrhtu, gryre.*
'peril, fear'
(*egesa*, 'danger, terror, dread')

eorδu   n. fem. *n*-stem *iþō*-stem, LR11 acc. sg.,
(eordu) CH(DP)5 gen. sg.

eorþlic, etc.; *ierþ, ierþling.*
–

eorþan tuddor Christ 688, *Genesis* 1402, etc.
= **folde, middangeard**; *molde*: ≠ **heofon**
'the earth'
(*eorþe*, 'earth, world, ground, soil')

LEYERLE   Thank you, Mr Ball, very much. I take it, in view of the hour and the progress of the discussion, that we would be well advised to proceed with the papers and have our generalized discussion at the end, lest we waste time on things which might be less profitable. Perhaps then, we could move on to Professors Bailey and Robinson if you will, since I think that Mr Ball's remarks will move quite naturally into discussion material.

BAILEY–   In his keynote speech to the 1964 Literary Data Processing Conference,
J. ROBINSON   Professor Fogel of Cornell spoke of the 'vision-actuality interval' that divides idea and product in science and scholarship. This sort of academic cultural lag can be quite short in science or technology; but in human pursuits, as Professor Fogel noted, the gap can be enormous.[6] Nowhere, we

6   E. G. Fogel, 'The Humanist and the Computer: Vision and Actuality,' *Literary Data Processing Conference, Proceedings,* eds. Jess B. Bessinger, Jr, Stephen M. Parrish, and Harry F. Arader (White Plains, N.Y., 1965), pp. 11-24.

suppose, is execution so maddeningly slow as in painstaking historical lexicography. Three-quarters of a century were needed for the Philological Society's *New English Dictionary* (now better known as the OED), and the final fascicle of several on-going dictionaries promises to be long in coming. However clearly we can foresee our visionary Old English dictionary, we will need plenty of patience before the actuality is realized.

Having stated what seems to us a gloomy truth, we must quickly add that we believe current technology has a good deal to offer the lexicographer beyond the now commonplace – and most helpful – provision of lexical concordances. Though we have certainly had discouraging moments in our encounters with the machine, we feel convinced that the computer can offer the scholarly lexicographer a variety of useful aids that will take some of the harmful drudgery out of his task. Perhaps we can give a more vivid idea of what functions might be turned over to the machine by describing our current work on the renascent Early Modern English dictionary. Since this conference marks our first public discussion of this work, let us begin with a short history of the project.

In 1928, work began at the University of Michigan on a dictionary of the Early Modern period intended to take its place in the series of period and regional dictionaries first proposed by Sir William Craigie in 1919 and now partially realized in the *Middle English Dictionary,* the *Dictionary of the Older Scottish Tongue,* the *Scottish National Dictionary,* and the *Dictionary of American English.*[7] Professor Charles C. Fries, the first editor of the proposed EMED and its editor until his death in 1967, intended to produce a comprehensive record of the English language 'used from 1475 to 1700 – that is, from the beginning of printing in England until the death of Dryden.'[8]

As a first step in assembling a collection adequate to support such a dictionary, Professor Fries obtained the citation slips for Early Modern English which had been collected by readers and editors of the OED. Further collecting was done by volunteers – mainly in the United States – and by members of Fries' staff. Still other additions were purchased for the collection – for example, the special collection of agricultural words made by F. R. Ray, a one-time assistant on the OED staff. Early work on the dictionary proceeded from collecting to editing, and Professor Fries and his associates produced sample copy for the letter *l* for the then intended publisher of the work,

---

7 See Sir William A. Craigie, 'New Philological Schemes Presented to the Philological Society, 4th April, 1919,' *Transactions of the Philological Society, 1925-1930* (1931), 6-11; Charles C. Fries, Sir William A. Craigie, *et al.,* 'The Period Dictionaries,' *PMLA*, XLVII (1931), 890-97; Sir William A. Craigie, 'The Value of the Period Dictionaries,' *Transactions of the Philological Society*, XIX (1937), 53-62.

8 The most comprehensive published history of the EMED appears in *The University of Michigan: An Encyclopedic Survey* (Ann Arbor, 1943), pp. 570-73.

the Oxford University Press. But the 1930s were not a happy time for historical lexicography. The financial support that had previously been granted to lexicography at Michigan was much diminished by the end of the decade, and, furthermore, important differences of opinion arose between the editors in Ann Arbor and the English publisher concerning the scope and style of the dictionary. Finally, in 1939, work on the dictionary was indefinitely postponed so that editorial and financial resources might be concentrated on the *Middle English Dictionary*. Though the delay was thought to be only temporary, the war years made immediate resumption of work impossible and what was to be respite turned into long slumber.

Thoughts of reviving the project turned to action in 1965 when members of the English department at Michigan under Professor Fries's direction began the difficult process of reassembling materials and files put in storage twenty-five years before. In the summer of 1967 a conference was held in Ann Arbor to survey opinions of linguists and literary scholars about the need for such a dictionary and to ask for advice about how it might be planned and executed. The participants in that conference from outside the university – Harold B. Allen, W. Nelson Francis, Henry A. Gleason, Jr, Philip B. Gove, Raven I. McDavid, Jr, and others – warmly urged the need for a dictionary of the period. More and more scholars are now becoming aware of this need, particularly as other dictionaries appear or are initiated on the Oxford plan: the handsome *Dictionary of Canadianisms on Historical Principles* ought certainly to be mentioned here, as should the *Dictionary of Jamaican English* and the proposed Australian dictionary. Craigie's vision is now half a century old and much of it has been realized; the Early Modern English dictionary is becoming more and more noticeable by its absence.

During the summer of 1968 we spent much of our time examining the citation file that is the most valuable legacy of Professor Fries's work a generation ago. From our examination of a sample of 20,000 slips, we estimate the file to contain just over three million usable citations. Something over half come from the OED collection; though many of them are more than a century old, they are in sound condition, however unsuitable they may be for even the most visionary of optical scanners. The rest of the slips are mostly the result of the work of Professor Fries and the volunteer readers of the thirties. Many of these are cut from photocopies of selected Renaissance texts and, unlike the handwritten slips, are unquestionably accurate. During our summer's work, we discovered a great variety of information about the composition of our file: the kinds of works excerpted, the adequacy of the context provided, the representation of words from technical vocabularies, the distribution of material through the period, and so on. All this information seems most encouraging to us: we feel that the citation file is a uniquely valuable resource that could not be economically reproduced even if by some stroke of magic every text in our period were translated into machine-readable form.

Important differences exist between our task and that foreseen for an Old English dictionary. Most significant, we believe, is the sheer impossibility of examining all the texts in our period for all the extant uses of a given form. Yet lexicography is so concerned with the particular that statistical sampling techniques seem inappropriate for such work. We would not willingly subscribe to a policy that would exclude any usage or form from consideration, yet it is in practice impossible for us to estimate confidently the margin of error for the collection upon which the dictionary depends. Somehow we must come to terms with this difficulty and define the point at which collection gives way to editing.

Other problems come to mind and, though we cannot give them extensive treatment here, we would welcome your counsel. Is the OED plan, for instance, the best one for historical lexicography today? Venerable as it is, we feel that it should be thoroughly re-examined before we embark on an EMED.[9] Further, what should be the relation between linguistic and encyclopaedic information in a modern historical dictionary? Should an EMED attempt to extend the extra-linguistic information provided in the OED or should we emulate the more severe policy of the *Middle English Dictionary* in this respect? Most important to us are questions concerning the relation of contemporary linguistic theory to practical lexicography. Historical linguistics, is, after all, becoming the subject of thoroughgoing examination from several quarters and a plan for a new dictionary must acknowledge new views. Half a century of structuralism – broadly conceived – has had practically no effect on dictionary making, though it has revolutionized other aspects of language study. Now that we are faced with the opportunity of fixing a plan for a major new dictionary, we believe that the familiar scheme of our historical dictionaries should be subject to some strenuous criticism before we begin a new reference work either for Old or for Early Modern English.[10]

9 Professor Hans Aarsleff has done much to clarify the intellectual history of the OED, though we would welcome more information about the smaller editorial decisions that gave rise to the familiar format. In particular it would be useful to examine in detail the 'specimen of what I thought a dictionary ought to be' prepared by Murray when, singlehandedly, he began to revive the almost moribund dictionary after Furnivall withdrew as editor in 1878. See Aarsleff's 'The Early History of the *Oxford English Dictionary*,' *Bulletin of the New York Public Library*, LXVI (1962), 417-39; and *The Study of Language in England, 1780-1860* (Princeton, 1967). The subsequent history of the work is sketched informally in *Sir James A. H. Murray: A Self-Portrait*, ed. George F. Timpson (Eastgate and Gloucester: John Bellows Ltd., 1957).

10 Competing views on diachronic linguistics are particularly interesting for the historical lexicographer. See, for instance, Paul Kiparsky, 'Linguistic Universals and Linguistic Change,' in *Universals in Linguistic Theory*, eds. Emmon Bach and

Finally, we have wondered if we ought to be aiming at a printed volume of the familiar sort at all. Perhaps we should anticipate that query-answering machine which is supposed to provide the future scholar with the wisdom of mankind at the touch of a button. Our conclusion is not as sanguine on that issue as is that of some academic visionaries, but we do endorse the opinion of Professor Josselson when he says that provision should be made for the machine-storable reference work at the same time that the printed version is produced.[11] In other words, we believe that books are not yet obsolete, but we want to hedge our bet.

Until very recently, lexicographers have been proudly innocent of technology, and dictionary offices nowadays differ little from the courts of Alexandria where the Homeric texts were examined in the third century BC. Even commercial dictionaries have followed in this conservative – if hallowed – tradition, the advertising for the recent *Random House Dictionary* notwithstanding.[12] Even when lexicographers have turned to machines like automatic typesetters or digital computers, they have asked that these devices be adapted to traditional practices. Concordances, of course, are a convenient meeting ground between a familiar scholarly tool and the simpler capacities of the computer, so it is no surprise that they have been the most popular product of literary and linguistic data processing. Perhaps equally obvious to the lexicographer is the possibility of producing citation slips of the usual kind. The concordance principle can easily be adapted to this output and, in Britain and the United States, such slips have been produced on a large scale for the dictionary of the *Older Scottish Tongue* and, more modestly, for the *Middle English Dictionary*.[13] In our

Robert T. Harms (New York, 1968), pp. 170-202; and Uriel Weinreich, William Labov, and Marvin I. Herzog, 'Empirical Foundations for a Theory of Language Change,' in *Directions for Historical Linguistics: A Symposium,* eds. W. P. Lehmann and Yakov Malkiel (Austin, Texas, 1968), pp. 95-188.

11　Harry H. Josselson, 'Lexicography and the Computer,' in *To Honour Roman Jakobson: Essays on the Occasion of His Seventieth Birthday* (The Hague, 1967), vol. II, pp. 1046-59.

12　In his preface to the college edition of the RHD, the editor speaks warmly of electronic data processing. However the use of such devices in the preparation of that work was intellectually and practically quite minor: see Laurence Urdang's 'The Use of Typographic Coding in Information Retrieval,' in *Progress in Information Science and Technology: Proceedings of the American Documentation Institute 1966* (Santa Monica, 1966), pp. 193-200; and 'The Systems Designs and Devices Used to Process *The Random House Dictionary of the English Language,' Computers and the Humanities,* I (1966), 31-3.

13　Work at the DOST is described by A. J. Aitken and Paul Bratley, 'An Archive of Older Scottish Texts for Scanning by Computer,' *Studies in Scottish Literature,* IV (1966), 45-7. At the University of Michigan, the system for producing slips has been designed by William Ingram and Victor J. Streeter.

own work, slips have been produced for texts by Sidney and Milton. (We should not fail to mention the generosity of William A. Elwood of the University of Virginia and William Ingram of the University of Michigan who gave us free access to the materials that they have converted to machine-readable form at considerable expense and trouble.) The ready availability of texts in our period has thus allowed us to add significantly to the citation file for the EMED at relatively little cost. With so many texts in Old English now becoming available in computer form, the editors of an Old English dictionary can look to uses of the computer that are uneconomical for the EMED.

Even the production of slips by computer, however, brings with it certain problems that the lexicographer may not at first anticipate. The reduction of variants to canonical form, the distinction of homographs, and the proper selection of phrasal entries all prove to be vexing problems that a human volunteer would soon master. The witless computer can be made to master most of them, but a good deal of programming is required before the results become relatively acceptable. Likewise the lexicographer may find himself inundated with bales of slips unless he has cleverly designed a list of excluded words. But even then, the nagging doubt remains that some treasured form may be disposed of in the winnowing process.

Other aspects of lexicography could well profit from the use of the computer without altering the traditional procedures. Dictionary makers, after all, spend a good deal of time preparing text for the typesetter and correcting proof; such work is now a necessary but vexing use of the lexicographer's time. Future projects might well take inspiration from the Wycliffe Bible translators' system in Mexico City. There, sixteen consoles will, when the system is completely operating, function simultaneously as the Bible translators type, correct, alter, and right-justify testaments with the aid of a relatively inexpensive computer installation. Through this system, the annual output of the centre will be doubled – to 12,000 pages per year! – and much more efficient use will be made of the very special skills of the translators.[14] Since the lexicographer's time is no less expensive – and his skills no less exotic – than that of the specialist in aboriginal languages, we believe that it would be unconscionable to begin a new dictionary project without making the fullest use of such dull but precious applications of computers.

The uses of data processing equipment just mentioned are novel in most dictionary projects, but we should not fail to mention an undertaking in

14 According to a report justifying the value of the system: 'the time Institute members in Mexico alone lose from concentrated effort on other things because they are waiting out publication delays can be estimated conservatively at 50 man months per year, and probably costs the Christian public $10,000 a year.' Further information on this system can be obtained from Joseph E. Grimes of the Summer Institute of Linguistics.

which they occupy a central role in lexicography, the *Trésor de la langue française* under the direction of M Paul Imbs at Nancy. This work aims to supply France with historical dictionaries on the grandest of scales; when completed, the work will consist of two alphabets covering the language from Old French through 1950. What is most impressive is the fact that 250 million words will be used as the data base upon which the work will be built. Automatic production of citation slips is now underway, and thirty-eight operators are hard at work simply preparing text for the Gamma 60 computer installation at the project headquarters. In these ambitious plans, we can see an attempt to compress the history of English lexicography into the period between 1960 and the scheduled completion date, 1980. Bibliographical and textual work is now being undertaken that will bear the same relation to the *Trésor* that the Early English Text Society has had to the OED and the *Middle English Dictionary*. The computer at Nancy takes the place of the myriad of volunteer readers available to the OED in building the citation file. Editing the dictionary, however, will still be carried out in the traditional way, though the editor's ability to retrieve disparate supporting evidence will be far greater than that of other lexicographers.[15]

Since the EMED is already supplied with an excellent citation file very much like the one that M Imbs and his associates are trying to construct, we have investigated some of the ways in which the machine might be even more useful to us in the editorial work that we face. The example of the *Dictionary of American Regional English* at Madison suggested man-machine interaction as one direction in sharing editorial work with the computer, and we began to wonder if we might not be able to justify the enormous cost of transferring our three million slips to machine-readable form. At first we were enthralled by this heady vision. But eventually we decided that for our work the computer should be relegated to ancillary tasks since the sheer volume of complex material makes editing the EMED by computer far more complicated than is the case with the *Dictionary of American Regional English* or an Old English dictionary. Even assuming the most conservative estimates, the expense of converting our materials to the computer would exceed a million dollars and the additional cost of computer time for on-line editing would be substantial. Though we are convinced that this decision is correct in view of the state of lexicography and of technology today, let us conclude by describing some current work that can be said, we hope, to anticipate the unforeseen in computational lexicography.

After two decades of attempts at machine translation, few believe that automatic semantic analysis of texts by computer is immanent. This is, of

15 Perhaps the most accessible description of the work at Nancy is to be found in the descriptive brochure distributed by the Bureau des relations extérieures et de l'information du Centre national de la recherche scientifique entitled: *Centre de recherche pour un trésor de la langue française.*

course, the view of Professor Bar-Hillel and others who have had considerable experience in computational linguistics.[16] Nevertheless, we share the
view of Professor Josselson and John Olney that potentially interesting
information on the semantic structure of language can emerge from the
study of co-occurrence patterns in dictionaries themselves.[17] To this end,
we have nearly completed the preparation of C. T. Onions's *Shakespeare
Glossary* for the computer and hope before very long to make comparisons
between the behaviour of words in the glossary and in Shakespeare's plays.
Perhaps our version of this lexicon may prove useful to other computer-
aided studies of Renaissance texts and we invite other scholars to make use
of it.

With the sad history of machine translation behind them, linguists interested in the computer have turned their attention to possible interaction
between man and machine. Programs to test the rules of phonology or syntax are becoming more widely available, and more ambitious projects to
assist linguistic field workers have been proposed. It was natural, then, for
us to begin to explore ways in which the defining process itself might be
facilitated through the use of the computer. With encouragement from Dr
Walter A. Reitman, we have induced an experienced lexicographer – John
Reidy, associate editor of the *Middle English Dictionary* – to appear at the
University's Mental Health Research Institute. Citation slips, previously encoded in a machine-readable file, appear on a small television screen and
the lexicographer writes a provisional definition for the cited usage on the
screen by means of a typewriter keyboard. Corrections and alterations can
easily be made at any time and the slips in the file for a given entry form
can be rapidly displayed. After having studied the slips, the lexicographer
can write the final definition and link the slips to each of the senses he has
discriminated. Were the operation of such a system economical, it would be
quite possible to produce an abridged version of the dictionary containing
no citations (parallel to the *Shorter Oxford*) or to make available any desired amount of detail up to and including the entire contents of the citation
file with its accompanying definitions. Such flexibility is evidently desirable,
and, coupled with the possibility of continual revision and expansion of the
reference work, the advantage of this approach to lexicography is fully evi-
dent. The main obstacle to implementation of the system, may we repeat,
is the cost of putting our many slips in machine-usable form. The system

16   See, for example, Yehoshua Bar-Hillel, 'The Outlook for Computational Semantics,' in *Proceedings of the Conference on Computer Related Semantic Analysis*
(1965), ed. Harry H. Josselson (Detroit: Wayne State University, n.d.).

17   Olney and his associates at System Development Corporation are working on a
study of *Webster's New Collegiate Dictionary, Seventh Edition.* See John Olney,
Carter Revard, and Paul Ziff, 'Processor for Machine-Usable Version of Webster's
at SDC, '*The Finite String*, IV, 3 (March 1967), 1-2.

itself uses relatively inexpensive hardware and can be operated at the tolerable cost of seven to ten dollars an hour.[18]

Before leaving this heady topic, we might add that a new version of the program just described will retain in a separate memory all the false starts and clever insights that the lexicographer produces while using the system. Such information is of no interest to the dictionary user, of course, but it does have value to Dr Reitman and his associates whose ulterior motive in helping us is to gain some knowledge of the lexicographer's cognitive processes. Though we are far from thinking that the machine will ever simulate the lexicographer's task, we do share the curiosity of the cognitive psychologists who would like to learn more about this special approach to problem solving.

Within the past few years we have seen the emphasis in humanistic computing change from data manipulation to interactive devices of the sort designed by Dr Reitman. For the benefit of practical lexicography, we hope to see the continued improvement of such systems and their everyday use by dictionary makers. But we can also expect to move beyond this visionary stage to an even more direct confrontation with the mechanisms underlying the material itself, the data recorded in historical dictionaries. Already one experimenter has formulated a simple mathematical model for language change[19] and we expect that the most interesting uses of the computer in the future will lie in the development of such models.

Returning for a moment to the present, we would like to endorse Professor Venezky's proposal for an Old English materials centre. Hopefully this plan can be executed within an even larger framework of a clearinghouse for lexicographical information. W. P. Lehmann of the University of Texas has suggested such a centre, and the new committee for lexicography of the MLA will apparently lend its support to an international repository for English lexicography in which the materials that have been used in word indices, concordances, and historical dictionaries can be gathered.[20] Such a collection may eventually foster even greater co-operation in turning our hopes for better dictionaries to actuality. Thank you.

18 An account of the system used in this experiment can be found in a paper by Walter A. Reitman, R. Bruce Roberts, Richard W. Sauvain, and Daniel D. Wheeler, 'AUTONOTE: A Personal Information Storage and Retrieval System,' Ann Arbor: Mental Health Research Institute, Communication no. 248 (March 1969).

19 Sheldon Klein, 'Historical Change in Language Using Monte Carlo Techniques,' *Mechanical Translation*, IX (1966), 67–82.

20 See Lehmann's concluding remark in his review of two recent etymological dictionaries, *College English*, XXVIII (1967), 628. The new MLA committee is chaired by Raven I. McDavid, Jr.

LEYERLE Thank you, Professor Bailey, for that illuminating and stimulating account.
F. ROBINSON I am afraid I am not competent to speak either as a lexicographer or as a
computist. The few remarks I have to make are merely the views of someone who is very interested in having a new Old English dictionary – if possible, in my lifetime – and so mine will be the least substantial of the pre-
sentations you are hearing this afternoon. I think, in fact, that I have been
sandwiched in as a kind of buffer of redundancy between the Bailey-Rob-
inson report and Professor Cameron's closing remarks, in which dense
quantities of information must be absorbed at an incredible rate. You can
relax for the next few minutes (or pages) and prepare yourselves for the
next onslaught of new information.

I was somewhat appalled yesterday to hear the history of calamities inci-
dent to humanists' efforts to use the computers. But maybe these blunders
that the machines make only go to show that computers are, after all, only
human, and that they are more engaging for being so. You may have read
recently about the machine translator which was directed to translate the
Biblical phrase 'The spirit is willing but the flesh is weak' from one language
or other into English. The machine came up with the translation 'The whis-
key is agreeable but the meat is poor.' I think we can muster more genuine
affection for that computer than we can for all the coldly efficient calcula-
tors in the world.

But machine errors of this kind are, of course, intolerable in the kind of
project which we are envisioning here and, if I have understood the drift of
the meeting yesterday and today, the main solution to problems involving
computers and the preparation of concordances is to be found in setting
up some kind of centre for pooling the experience of the people we have
heard today and of others not here who have been using computers in concording Old English texts. (In London Janet Bately has, I believe, been
using machines in her preparation of a concordance to the Old English
Orosius, and there are other concordances of Old English underway elsewhere.) If we could agree upon the establishment of such a centre, it would
certainly be a step forward for the dictionary project as a whole, and it
seems in fact to be a feasible step since the computists are already in a
much better organized state than are those of us who are primarily interested in the end product of our efforts, the dictionary itself. And therefore
I would like to suggest – since that is all I can do – that before this meeting
completely dissolves there should be some kind of caucus between Professor
Bessinger, if he is still here, Professor Venezky, the people from Michigan,
and the others to see exactly what form this Old English materials centre
should take. As for the form of the concordance itself which would result
ultimately from all this, it seems to me that this is still a somewhat open
issue. The remarks that Dr Mitchell has just made – in which he set forth so
skilfully the evils of a manuscript concordance which completely overlooks
the experience of years of excellent editing – were prepared, as he has

indicated, before he was able to hear the exposition we heard today in which it was explained that those preparing manuscript concordances would make a good deal of use of available editions, incorporating much information from them into the concordances after all. There might still be some question about where between these various methodologies the concorders will eventually find their actual operating principles, especially in their concording of texts which are as yet unedited or which have been imperfectly edited.

The second major need, as I understand it, is the establishment of a somewhat comparable centre for co-ordinating the work on the dictionary itself. It has been suggested that the MLA might be instrumental in this respect, and it was, in fact, at the October meeting of the officers of the Old English Group in New York that the current dictionary project was first formulated in the United States. Probably the MLA can continue to offer scholars on this side of the Atlantic a convenient means of coming together and discussing the problems of preparing the dictionary. But whether the MLA can offer anything more remains, so far as I know, an open question. And it's not even certain that the MLA can offer us a meeting place in the future, in fact. Owing to certain strange events at the last meeting in December, we were told for a time that there may be no meeting at all this year, and although the most recent communication from the Executive Secretary reports that there will now be a 1969 meeting in Denver, we have no assurance that we can look forward to regular meetings after 1969. It is possible, as some have suggested, that money might be forthcoming from MLA, but if it is I have no knowledge of it.

Being realistic, though, I would say that we should not think in terms of organizations like MLA, but should rather try to find out who the committed, industrious individuals will be who would enjoy the support of all Old Anglists in the world and who could move ahead on the actual work for the dictionary. Various groups in the United States and abroad have elected boards of editors and directors and committees of people who have a sort of paternal and advisory interest in the project, but it seems to me that it is now time for us to locate the actual people who will be prepared to devote the next two decades or so of their lives to the hard labour of compiling the dictionary. And these people must have behind them a university or some institution which will support their work. Once these editors are identified, then the rest of us can occupy more comfortably, it seems to me, our subordinate roles as diffident counsellors, moral supporters, and lexicographical drones. There is a great deal of talent in all these categories, of course, throughout the English-speaking world. Mr Ball's comments, it seems to me, are particularly good in this connection and I can only applaud his suggestion that we determine who the people are that are really going to get down to deciding the shape and nature of this dictionary and who would be able to move ahead with it. Maybe I could again suggest that there be some sort of caucus before we have a diaspora here, a caucus from which would emerge a number of people who would be capable and prepared to go ahead with the project. I can't even anticipate how the dictionary work would be organized, but it seems possible that it would take the form of a drone system in which there will be a large number of people working for a very small board of editors who would scrutinize their work and put it in proper form.

This raises some questions about where this talent would come from – that is, these highly qualified drones who would do specialized work in preparing material for the editors, who would then put it in final dictionary form. I have been compiling a list of people at work in Old English in the world who seem to me to have demonstrated an interest and talent in Old English word study and who would be very good for supporting jobs if they could only be persuaded to contribute a significant amount of their scholarly time to a dictionary project. What could you offer these highly trained and overworked professors and students of Old English for their services? My first thought is of the remark made by that nineteenth-century German monarch whose policies drove many professors (including Jakob Grimm) from their posts at the great German universities. When this royal personage was asked how he intended to replace the professors, he answered, 'Professoren, Huren und Ballettänzerinnen kann man für Geld überall haben.' But we have no money that I know of, and I doubt in any case whether money would really be the most attractive lure for the kind of people we need. Anyone who is competent in this exacting specialty is also, I am sure, eager to see the dictionary finished, and willing, if possible, to help with creating it.

But here we encounter various difficulties in various regions of academia. In the United States, deferring one's individual scholarly recognition by immersing oneself in a vast and anonymous dictionary project would be a prohibitively costly sacrifice for the individual embarking on an academic career in English philology. I have been discussing this obvious difficulty with some people here. Professor Stanley has suggested, among other things, that perhaps a concurrent monograph series could be set up alongside the dictionary project, and some of the material that scholars would be preparing for the dictionary would be published in monograph form in this series. This is a most promising idea. If an Old English yearbook of some kind materializes, it seems to me that this too could be quite useful: it could make regular reports on the dictionary project and could help give to the people working at all levels on the dictionary project the recognition and esteem that they would deserve.

Looking back at scholarly publications in the past which could be utilized in preparing the dictionary, I believe that the suggestion which Professor Cameron of Toronto made some months ago was a good one: he felt that a bibliography of lexicographical studies should be prepared prior to beginning the dictionary and perhaps incorporated into it. It seems to me that it would be a particularly good thing to prepare this bibliography before deciding the question that Professor Venezky mentioned, the question of determining stop words in making the concordances. For in deciding what the stop words are to be, we should perhaps first consider which Old English words have been studied so thoroughly already in monograph or book form that we could dispense with hundreds of pages of computer-gathered quotations for those words. For example, in deciding whether the computers should be directed to collect the myriad occurrences of Old English 'ān,' one should perhaps take into account the recent monograph by Matti Rissanen of Helsinki, *The Uses of One in Old and Early Middle English.*[21] In the light of Dr Rissanen's work, we might well be inclined to make 'ān' a stop word since a good dictionary entry could probably be compiled from his excellent monograph. At the same time, we must ask whether earlier publications would allow the editors to take into account all the subtleties that Mr Ball was envisioning so imaginatively and usefully as possibly going into the entries for a truly modern dictionary.

The problem of editing unedited texts and of whether editions should precede the concordance, which must precede the dictionary – all this, I would say, must remain an open question until it is determined just what form the concordances will take. But, in any case, the text-editing committee which has been set up and which people on both sides of the Atlantic seem to view favourably is in itself a good and useful institution. And since even a manuscript concordance would, as we have heard, incorporate a great deal of information from good editions, it would seem important that we move ahead with the editing so long as the talent and leadership are available.

There are one or two more things I would like to suggest as possible by-products of a great lexicographical project such as the one we are planning. For when we draw on so many people and such potent machines, we must move deliberately and make certain that we are not overlooking possibilities as we plan our data-collecting. A complete Old English frequency list has been mentioned; that is an obvious thing. It would certainly be a mistake to have all this Old English on calculating machines without using them to gather that easily accessible information. A backwards word list, a flip concordance, would be useful also, and perhaps the concordance programs could be made to include directions for this. And perhaps now is the time to consider another project that has never really gotten much attention at all but which would be useful – an English-Old English dictionary. Possibly there is some way that our material for the Old English dictionary could be keyed for subsequent conversion to this form. And there are many other things, I am sure, that will be considered by the editorial committee as it deliberates so carefully on what sort of dictionary, finally, we will have.

21   Mémoires de la société néophilologique de Helsinki, 31 (Helsinki, 1967).

That's the extent of my redundant buffer remarks. For a more authoritative discussion of our problems, I suggest you brace yourself now for the absorption of heavy masses of information again.

LEYERLE I wonder, then, if at the risk of over-shaping the discussion, and in view of the shortage of time, if you will allow me again to make a summary. I will admit that what follows will be interpretive. We have reached a position where it is becoming clear that the various aspects of work we have been discussing are in fact so interrelated that it is very difficult to separate them. We have an over-all dictionary committee of Helmut Gneuss, Alistair Campbell, and a third member, yet to be appointed; a computistics committee headed by Professor Bessinger; an editorial committee cis-Atlantic, with Professors Collins, Irving, and Rosier; a European editorial committee with Alistair Campbell as chairman, Bruce Mitchell as secretary, and five other members. The points have been made repeatedly that whatever we do on one side of the work must reflect thought and care on the other sides: the computistics men have told us repeatedly that they need accurate thinking before they can set up a program, the lexicographical people have expressed interest in what sort of information should be available to them, and the editorial people have views on what kind of texts should be the basis for the dictionary. One other word that has been mentioned here but hasn't been articulated as a point – a task I think I should undertake – is the subject of linguistics. It is clear from what Mr Ball and Professor Bailey said, that linguistics is something which cannot be neglected; we would be ill-advised, I believe, to proceed only on the basis of traditional philological investigation without making full use of the last half-century of linguistic studies. Professor Clemoes has argued very convincingly that we must pay great attention to the texts we use, and others have supported this point. Mr Ball has shown that we must establish lexicographical criteria; Professor Bailey has held out the very attractive hope that the actual compilation of the dictionary can be done by mechanical process which would give us an extraordinarily flexible system, at surprisingly low cost. We are now discussing how best we could co-ordinate an activity which it is very difficult to separate into independent parts.

To conclude. What is implicit here – if I may now make the suggestion – is that we are talking about some kind of a new Old English group, which is not related particularly to the MLA or to a European body, but in fact to a world-wide group of Old English scholars united in a common purpose. I admit that this is a rather interpreted summary, but I would offer it as a basis now for discussion from the floor.

CROSS I think I'd like to support you immediately on that. Indeed I wonder if there might be a certain amount of false modesty among the institutions which might support such a centre. I suppose there are not many in England

which could, but it seems to me that perhaps there is money here somewhere, and perhaps one university is holding back in favour of another because it is being a little modest. I wonder if there are any universities here
which are prepared to be the centre for such a group? Whether they would
like to state this? Then we could proceed; there might be a hope for this
group. This is almost the most important thing in my mind, that we can
meet sometime again – those who are really interested.

CUMMINGS I think that I can speak for the University of Waterloo, that the humanities
faculties there and the Computing Centre would be most glad to entertain
in any way that it could any projects connected with the Old English concordances or the dictionary, making its facilities available; financing is
something I can't commit the university on, but the access to the facilities
is there if we want it, and the encouragement that we have received in our
efforts – Professor Logan and others and myself – from our university has
been open and generous. I think that if we decided to do something there
we could work with a minimum of friction, with whatever other kinds of
organizations or committees or centres we might generate. Also I think that
the forward-looking character of the people in the Computing Centre would
make them quite willing to work in some sort of a consortium with other
computing centres, to provide greater computing and sorting facilities.

BAILEY It seems to me that, as we look back at the history of the use of the computer, we see that people tend to get locked into a certain idea about how
the machine works. To begin with people thought, well, we'll use card
sorting devices simply to calculate statistical information of various sorts,
and so some rather clever plans were set up to enable people to sort the
physical cards in these ways. If we look at this French work which is
described in this illustrated booklet (the brochure on the Trésor project;
see p. 100, n. 15) we find they are producing an incredible number of citation slips on the concordance principle. Now for Old English it seems to
me this might be tolerable; for their project it is not, I think. They just
have more materials than they will ever be able to use sensibly, I suspect,
and the thrust of my remarks now is that you should not limit yourselves
to the idea of a gigantic concordance of all the extant Old English texts
and that's the end of the use of the machine. Obviously it is a good practical suggestion now, but I would encourage people to think of some of the
further uses the computer might be put to beyond the concordance.

SMITH Well, I couldn't agree more. I've always assumed that you would have a
dictionary in the computer as a group, that is, you would have these items
in computer form, and keep adding to them; whether you print from that
is irrelevant at the moment. The computer is not only going to give you a
concordance but it is going to do a lot of the housekeeping and the secretarial work.

MERRILEES Spade work!

SMITH Maybe spade work, yes, but there is a lot of spade work left to the scholars too. But a lot of the secretarial work, I would assume, will be done by the computer. It's the best way to keep these files; much better than any slips, at any stage of the game.

BAILEY Right. But that wasn't obvious in 1960, when this French project was designed and ten years hence maybe things that aren't obvious now will be standard practice.

SMITH I'm glad you brought it up.

PILLSBURY It sounds as if they had not made the distinction between a concordance and a lexicon, or as if they were conceiving of the lexicon on a concordance principle with no principle of elimination involved.

BAILEY Well, it is hard to tell. But there is an interesting picture in the brochure which appears to be just one bank of some thousand file drawers containing slips. That is just one row!

F. ROBINSON I'd like to say again, at the risk of being officious as well as redundant, that it would be well if people would come forward and make some kind of concrete statements about their active interest and about what they are willing to put into the dictionary project. I wonder if it would be possible to suggest that, after this meeting Professor Cummings and the Michigan people and Venezky and Dr Smith should get together and openly discuss the question of the computer co-ordinating centre and so on, and that their example might then be followed by an open, frank discussion of this other element we need so badly; the actual editors of the dictionary. This would result in the decision as to who the actual working people who are going to put the dictionary together, or plan the dictionary and so on, might be.

CROSS When I was thinking about this at first I asked two of my young colleagues whether they would like to help. I think this is the way it ought to be done, that the more senior people might be able to suggest colleagues whom they would consider to be competent. I think we have to be careful about volunteers – I'm sorry to appear rude but there must be some kind of statement in this way. I would think that in England there would be quite a few people who are not writing very much but who are competent Anglo-Saxonists, and if they thought – and if the suggestion went forward – that these unpublished homilies could be produced in the occasional papers of such and such a university, which was actually willing to print them, then it would give them some encouragement to do the work. They could have their names at the top of the homilies, and perhaps these could be passed round and somebody might say: 'Well, I know the source of that' and this could be added as an appendix. This might well take us forward rather quickly. Our attitude should be thought of in terms of those here who perhaps are not the 'drones' or workers – who aren't prepared actually to transcribe – but know of good competent colleagues who may be doing nothing very much or nothing terribly exciting at the moment. One of the reasons why we haven't got these homilies published was that certainly up until recently if you transcribed a homily, even edited it, you would never

get it published unless you had a source. Now a young man will probably
not find a source. He may not have the experience in knowing where to
look. But the occasional paper idea would allow various kinds of Anglo-
Saxonists to contribute. Sweet, Skeat, and the other great nineteenth-
century editors had their amanuenses.

STANLEY   I had in mind two rather different kinds of things to go into a monograph
series; on the one hand editions of the kinds Professor Cross has just mentioned, which are not in a way really final editions of permanent, scholarly
value but would be useful working material, and secondly the kind of thing
that has emerged recently, especially from Germany where the semantic
field theory, variously (and sometimes too mystically) conceived, has led to
a number of very good coherent studies of groups of words. I thought of
those two areas for these monographs because that would make it possible
for the heads of departments – who have to press for promotion for their
people – to be able to say that something is being done. Whereas one is
always under pressure as a junior lecturer to publish something in a definite
form, a kind of half-way house. There are a number of people, including
myself, who would be willing to put in some work; whether I would wish
to spend my remaining years on the project *in toto,* I don't want to say, but
I think at some time one might wish to produce something of this type.

CROSS   Part of the difficulty in the past was that there has been no glamour about
homilies. The younger people (and I was one) always want to produce *the*
great interpretation of *Beowulf,* or other things of that kind. But I think
we could give some sort of glamour to it by saying this is for the dictionary,
and for the dictionary will be forever.

F. ROBINSON   Somewhat like the Early English Text Society.

BELL   Could I make some general comments along the line of what you were saying about what we would like to see happen in Old English? This doesn't
apply too specifically to either concordances or the dictionary. But there
are three or maybe two and a half possible topics of future discussion I
don't think are covered too thoroughly here. One is what I call, for want
of a better term, prudent computation, or creative error – something like
that. The sort of thing that Professor Bailey was talking about in terms of
computers – aid in the defining process itself. One of the many types of
schizophrenia induced by exposure to computers in the humanities is the
spectrum between heavily pre-edited input and completely unedited input.
When you talk to most programmers they will usually give you, like a litany,
the dictum that you must know about questions you want to ask the computer. (This philosophy tends to promote pre-editing.) On the other hand,
if you ask many of them how they learned to become programmers they
very often say 'I just had a lot of time to fool around the machine.' It
seems to me that there is a place for both these extremes – the highly
instructive, trial-and-error fooling around by an untrained scholar helped
by a programmer, and the sophisticated project with more arcane goals,

usually employing pre-edited input. The importance of the former is that it provides lower-level points of entry for untrained scholars; yet my impression is that this approach is given low priority when resources are allocated. As an example of the importance of this approach even in sophisticated projects, I might mention Roy Wisbey's observations on 'crude computation' in connection with his work on Middle High German: if your goal is an automatic parsing program for a dictionary or grammatical analysis, the parsing parameters can be much better defined when the raw material has been 'crudely' pre-processed (e.g., concorded). In other words, 'crude' projects (1) are operationally useful and (2) provide untrained scholars with a chance to get their hands dirty and learn something. (I have subsequently found this to be true in a Middle English seminar: I had my students keypunch much of *Piers Plowman* for a simple concordance project and brought the programmer to class to discuss the project.) Another topic is pedagogical aids, which I think follow from some of Professor Robinson's comments. It seems to me that Old English has enough intrinsic merit that it doesn't have to be the sort of coterie, strictly graduate-level study that it is in too many American universities. If we had more pedagogical aids along the lines of Mrs Hieatt's recent grammar[22] or Ken Chapman's graded reading exercises in Old Icelandic,[23] we could create a more receptive audience to Old English studies on the undergraduate level. To give one example of the way the computer could contribute to this sort of thing; an unnamed and unknown-to-me friend of a programmer whom I know, is apparently going through Latin texts with certain parameters of simplicity to find out which parts of which text would be best to present in elementary and introductory courses in Latin. I think the same thing could very possibly be done with Old Norse or Anglo-Saxon.

Third, and this is probably a minor point, is the question of information exchange in the field in general, which I think ties in with questions which have been raised about copyright issues and our relations ultimately with publishers. I'm just a little concerned about the potential conflict between our best and worst instincts in this area, as exemplified by one man who did an extensive concordance for a major eastern university press. His own feeling about it was that he'd simply like to send the tape to anyone who had a concordance program that was compatible with it to let him run off his own. The publisher's feeling was that the enterprise was commercial as well, and that financial considerations had to be protected. I have a tape myself that I'd be quite willing to let anyone use, but I've had so much advice to keep my material to myself until I'm done that I'm beginning to doubt myself.

22 Constance B. Hieatt, *Essentials of Old English: Readings with Keyed Grammar and Vocabulary* (New York, 1968).
23 Kenneth G. Chapman, *Graded Readings and Exercises in Old Icelandic* (Berkeley, 1964).

Then, too, there's the issue of exchange of programs, and whether or not they should be copyrighted. One sees such a range between generosity and caginess. I'm just a little disturbed by the fact that these rules of thumb or protocol, or whatever you want to call them, don't seem to be sorting themselves out instinctively. Not that they could ever be imposed exactly or should be. But I think it's just another possibility.

CLEMOES   I wonder if I might just supplement my earlier remarks which were intended to bring out some of the difficulties of using manuscripts as raw material for dictionary making. What I should like to add are a few remarks in favour of using at least some printed editions as raw material. Some existing editions are, no doubt, entirely satisfactory for this purpose. Equally some are bad and would have to be discarded. What is important is that there is a great deal of middle ground. There are many existing editions which are not entirely satisfactory, but which, I would think, give a better starting point than going right back to the manuscripts, to rock bottom, as it were. A good example of this would be Skeat's edition of Aelfric's *Lives of the Saints*. I have myself had occasion to collate all the manuscripts of the *Lives* with the printed edition: I found that the main text was sound (except for the usual small scatter of minor errors) and the variants were unreliable. But it was no very great job, it wasn't an immense task, to mark in my copy all that I found in the manuscripts which the edition didn't show. I suppose that for these *Lives* there is something like an average of four, five, or six manuscripts extant to each item; in my opinion it's a much simpler method to revise a printed edition of this sort by collating it with the manuscripts than it would be to pass four, five, or six copies through the computer, independently. And I should have thought this was typical of a great many printed editions.

STANLEY   I think in addition to Dr Clemoes' own collations very many other scholars have at various times collated material and have it available. I know, for instance, of one full collation of Skeat's *Lindisfarne Gospels* with hundreds of errors, but only hundreds of errors as opposed to the thousands which a new transcription might well produce.

VENEZKY   Before we close, I would just like to ask those of you who have a copy of the proposal I wrote up who have comments to make; would you please either see me and make them orally, or jot them down and either send them to me at Wisconsin or give them to me here. I will attempt to revise this within whatever framework of a committee that we set up here.

LEYERLE   Could I focus attention on this point again. If we are to set up a committee, I think we ought not to delay much longer. Perhaps it's not your wish to do so ...

CROSS   I don't think we can go away without doing something.

BESSINGER   We have a number of committees. I need some clarification in my own mind on what other committees are wanted. We have a cis-Atlantic and a trans-Atlantic editorial committee; we have a computer committee, which is international; we have a proposal for an Old English materials centre which as yet has no geographic home but which might, I should think, if I may be bold, be located in or near Toronto where the new microfilm collection of all Old English manuscripts is being made. We have most generous prospects at Waterloo with those magnificent and otherworldly machines and the generosity of the people who control them there. We do need, perhaps, some co-ordinating body to keep all of these different bodies, at different levels and all aiming in different directions, in touch with each other; but I can't myself imagine what single governing committee or centre we could vote into being today which would have any reality, or which would have any funds funding it, or which would have any personnel attending it; personnel who could communicate with each other face-to-face, or by telephone, or anything practical like that. I would like instruction on what is wanted.

CROSS   I take it we are talking straight, are we? I'll be 3,000 miles away tomorrow so I think I can talk straight. I am not a member of MLA and I take it that very few of the continental people will be. As far as I understand it the MLA hasn't really come forward and helped us yet, have they?

BESSINGER   If you mean with money, they have not, and will not, and cannot.

CROSS   Will they?

BESSINGER   No; MLA has no money.

CROSS   No money?

BESSINGER   Not a cent. It never did; and should never be represented as having.

CROSS   I see. Well in this case we have to look elsewhere, don't we?

BESSINGER   Indeed, yes.

CROSS   In a sense, you put forward a slight proposal when you suggest that perhaps materials could be channelled through this university. I really feel we want somebody we can write to, or somebody who will write to us.

CAMPBELL   When Professor Leyerle suggested that we need some kind of a new Old English world organization, my heart leapt because this is the sort of thing we do need – some kind of centre around which the various committees are established, and to which ordinary people might want to communicate and contribute. I have no right to suggest that Toronto might offer, but since Canada is usually a very good half-way point, ideologically and politically, between the United States and England, this might be the place to set it up.

FARRELL   Would it not be better to propose someone who would act as secretary, as intermediary between all of these bodies, committees, and individuals? Someone in one place to whom one could write, offer aid, offer financial support, someone who perhaps could get financial support.

LEYERLE   I think perhaps I should just respond to the point Professor Bessinger made by saying that one of the reasons I thought this conference was important to hold was because it was becoming clear to me in conversations with many other people who are in this room and others who have written to me that there was some danger that we would be working at cross-purposes. I think that this was clear in the discussions here; we have had a variety of view-points which I think can be reconciled into creative activity; my point was not really that any of these committees should be supplanted or indeed that they should be done away with, only that I felt that there was a great need for co-ordination so that the channels of communication would be open in all directions and there would be some common sense of purpose in the direction that we take.

BESSINGER   It's a point I thoroughly subscribe to. May I presume, Mr Chairman, upon our old friendship to suggest that the Centre for Medieval Studies might be a good temporary locus for international communications, if it would not be an intolerable burden for you and your colleagues and your secretaries simply to act as a temporary and single-stage clearing house? Inter-communications on the subjects of this meeting are so various and so pregnant with future implications, dangers, expenses, and challenges, that I think we cannot do more than establish this clearing house. Would it be proper to make such a motion? Is that what you were inviting?

LEYERLE   No indeed, least of all.

BESSINGER   Then I will not make the motion to the table, or the chair, but leave it in the air. Perhaps it can be brought down by someone else and localized.

CROSS   Nevertheless, you see, it is very difficult if we go away and talk and some-body arranges something privately. You know this is often done after meet-ings. Somebody comes up and volunteers. But I'm not so certain whether this is a very happy situation, since we're all here together. It is difficult of course. But as I now understand it there are going to be three centres for medieval studies in this continent, and we haven't got any in Europe, and it must be, I think, one of these places. Once you set up a centre you take on a responsibility which is far wider.

MITCHELL   As I see it there's the practical problem. I mean, here we have, say, an edi-torial committee in Europe and we have an editorial committee on this side of the Atlantic – now what exactly are we going to do? Am I now supposed to write around to all the professors in England and say 'do you know any-body, for example, to deal with this point of Professor Stanley's about the collations.' Suppose I do produce a list of collations of manuscripts and so on, as Professor Clemoes suggested, well then I write to somebody. Now what power has anybody got to say to people 'OK, we are going to do it this way, or we are going to do it that way' and this is the real practical diffi-culty, isn't it?

BESSINGER   There is another practical difficulty, Mr Chairman. That is that the two dis-tinguished members of the dictionary committee mentioned by name this afternoon, whose names and whose glory I applaud, are not present, and we have been talking with great enthusiasm about the kind of dictionary they should compose! It seems to me to be a matter of human certainty and his-torical truth that these gentlemen are going to design their dictionary in the way they feel it should be designed and then ask us for help; I hope so –

they will certainly do the designing. Will they not? Will not Professor Campbell settle in his mind the grand designs of the new Old English dictionary, and then proceed?

MITCHELL   Well, I really don't know. I mean this is the real practical problem, isn't it? I agree that we haven't got anybody from this side of the Atlantic who is on the dictionary committee and I take it – I didn't make up the name of that – I think that is the name that has emerged from the proceedings of the MLA meeting.

BESSINGER   These men must be on the committee.

MITCHELL   Yes, they must be! But these gentlemen will have to meet somehow and whoever the American representative is, they will have to get together, but you may know more about this than I do.

F. ROBINSON   No, I was going to ask you. I gether that we are talking about Professor Gneuss, and Professor Campbell, and the American mystery member of the triumvirate. Do I understand it? I didn't realize it before, that these are working editors of the dictionary?

MITCHELL   No. I don't think this has been decided at all – I mean, in that sense; I take it that Professor Campbell in England and Professor Gneuss in Germany are the sort of grand patrons who are going to put everything they can behind the project, to get young people whom they know about, to keep things moving. This is encouragement, is it not? We do not expect them to act as editors.

STANLEY   I think so. There was no thought in their minds that the grand design of a dictionary should come from them. I think that the phrase indicates the distance between Professor Bessinger's thinking of their position and their own.

BESSINGER   But from whom, if not from them?

STANLEY   Those who will be working at it. It must come from those who are actually working at the material. I think that is where it will come.

BESSINGER   But they are going to be correlating and gathering material, are they not?

STANLEY   It was not expected, I'm quite certain, when we drew up the kind of head through whom contact with scholars might be established conveniently, that they should be the designers of the dictionary which certainly in our assumption was going to be largely on this side of the Atlantic, and perhaps in Toronto.

COLLINS   I think that the distance between Professor Stanley and Professor Bessinger can be somewhat bridged by this observation. It was my understanding that when these committees were first set up, they were set up as the nucleus of a committee. That a committee would expand itself, and I think that this is what you're saying, that if it doesn't start with these people, where is it going to start? And that they would expand it and then with the enlarged group, come up with a plan of action. And the design, by which all these committees were designed – I think the phrase is nuclear ...

REIDY   Assuming that the grand old men expand their committee and come up with a design, sooner or later, they'll have to appoint an editor-in-chief, and if I know anything about scholars, that editor-in-chief is going to do the dictionary the way he wants to do it, and he may or may not take any notice of the other people, however good their advice. And in any case, when he gets into it in practice he may find that some of the best ideas, ones that sounded awfully good, do not work so well and in any case – knowing scholars, one knows perfectly well that when you appoint an editor he will really decide what has to be done. Up 'til then the thing remains in potency but not in action.

RIGG   Can we ask if the London committee actually had in mind an editor?

MITCHELL   No. I don't think it felt called upon to have one. We were interested, enthusiastic, hopeful of seeing a dictionary, and we got together in the hope that we would ultimately be able to provide this sort of material, look around, find young people who could help.

CROSS   I think one has to remember the names, you see. We regard ourselves as an editorial committee. We will help as much as we can with the production of texts and this was why we made this proposal about helping to put material forward. But I do agree with John Reidy that we eventually have to name a man and he's not going to be an old man either.

LEYERLE   While you reflect on this matter, I would just like to raise one other brief and, I think, much more simply dealt-with question, and that is that, in the frame of reference of this conference, we planned to publish the proceedings, hence the tape machinery, and the care we've taken to get the voices attributed to a name. It is our hope to edit this material and publish it sometime within the near future, although please don't ask me to define what I mean by that. We hope that it will be published so that it will be useful in the discussions which will ensue from this conference. I don't know whether you would like to consider your editorial committee for these proceedings or not. I take it that for convenience it would probably have to be a local committee here, although I equally take it that we would probably circulate a preliminary transcript at least of the principal speakers so that they may have a chance to edit their remarks as they see fit. Would you care to express views on this? Well, if there is no discussion here, I take it that tacitly you leave this problem in our hands. Then perhaps we should revert to the other if you would care to bring it together beyond the point where we left it. It is now 5:30 and I think we really must end soon. I know some people have plane reservations and we also, of course, have a reception to go to if you care to.

STANLEY   Mr Cameron is still down to speak. I hope that his paper will be included in the transactions because of the general interest of the practical things that he has done, even though time has prevented him addressing us in person today.

CAMERON   Thank you, Professor Stanley. Again, I still don't have a paper up my sleeve, but I want to say that I do feel the urgency of our doing something at this particular moment about a concordance series, and about a dictionary and about a bibliography of word studies. I feel that this is really the chance of a lifetime, to begin work on an Old English dictionary. I hope that we won't miss the opportunity. I feel that because of the great response which you've given to this meeting, the interesting things you've said, the promptness with which you've come, the large numbers of you who've come, show that there is interest, and I feel that co-operation on an international scale for this sort of thing is possible. I hope it will come about before this meeting is over today.

FARRELL Would it be possible since we are all gathered here, either in the immediate or in proximate future, for each person at the conference to express what they would be interested in doing as a contribution towards the project. What names they might be able to give of other persons, junior colleagues, friends, people who have done work in the past who might care to contribute to this sort of thing, some kind of compendium, some index of who is willing, able, ready to help.

CAMPBELL To whom should that sort of thing be sent? We need a continuing committee. If we are to communicate we must have some centre. This is a good idea but it assumes what Bessinger and I were trying to get at – some kind of continuing committee or commitment to carry on temporarily the organization.

LEYERLE I take it you would like me to respond to your suggestion and the one Professor Bessinger made.

CAMPBELL Yes!

LEYERLE Well, I don't think I could really offer, on behalf of my colleagues, to undertake such a large task without consulting with them at the start. Secondly, I think there are financial implications in it which Professor Bessinger rightly touched on, and I would feel irresponsible, for my part, to accept even a temporary responsibility without ascertaining that the necessary finances were, if not in hand, at least in sight. I might say, though, just to put an encouraging light on this – for reasons which I won't go into – that there seems to be a fair prospect of support in Canada at the moment for group projects of an international nature, particularly those connected with computers and those which rely on interconnections between humanities and technical work. I think, in other words, there would be hope of foundation support. Even by articulating it, I worry that this hope may be misconstructed as in fact a promise, which it couldn't possibly be. Those would be the two points I would make. I feel that I'd have to have the views of Professor Cameron and Professor Shook and other Toronto people before undertaking such a commitment to co-ordinate this. I would, of course, also like to know the views of other individuals concerned, such as Professor Gneuss and Professor Campbell, who are not here, to make certain they felt that this was appropriate. Obviously, it's a delicate task and I feel very hesitant in undertaking it unless it really did have strong support. I also feel a little awkward; in organizing this conference, we might be supposed to have hoped that something like this might develop. Quite the reverse. We thought we were making our contribution in a one-time effort by bringing this group together. We hoped that others would go on with the job. I will have spoken with irony if that someone turns out to be one of Toronto's people.

CAMPBELL   Thank you. I didn't mean to press you rudely.

LEYERLE   I wonder if I could ask Professor Pope to comment on this, as I think we all know and perhaps should put on record, that he was the hoped-for American member but declined the responsibilities because of other commitments. I think we would welcome your views on this, sir.

POPE   Well, I don't know what I can say that will be helpful, although I've been meditating while you've been talking. I don't know whether it would be helpful to make this suggestion or not, but it's all I can come up with. I pass over the question whether I would be willing to help. If I live long enough, I certainly will be, but I don't want to commit myself to anything now because I have something else I have to do first. What I, just tentatively, have to suggest is this: that I can see nothing better for the moment than that Professor Leyerle be willing to receive correspondence on the subject of people's hopes and plans and willingnesses and so on, that he for the moment agree to act as intermediary. But the second thing that occurs to me as a possibility is that each one of the committees now in existence should make some effort, perhaps with Professor Leyerle's help, to come together, either as an entire group, or by means of representatives of each one of them, so that they could talk further in a rather business-like way about the co-ordination of the effort and the kind of people that should be appointed to do the biggest part of the work. That is all I can think of at the moment.

LEYERLE   Thank you, Professor Pope. That second suggestion is a very helpful one and, if we could get finances for it, I think that this would be one of the first orders of business, to get all the people concerned together in one place.

CUMMINGS   I'm thinking of this idea of trying to get some money to support our ambitions. Wouldn't it be better if somehow there was a body that the Canada Council or other foundation might be able to recognize? That's why I think there should be a connection with MLA or, failing that, that perhaps this group might constitute itself as an ad hoc group in some way and appoint some sort of a steering committee, persons who have heard all our concerns and our complicated interrelations to adjust these things, and at the same time, perhaps investigate the financial basis of our ambitions.

SHOOK   I'd like to rise, Mr Chairman, and say that I could pull a hundred million out of my pocket, but I can't. But it does seem to me that since the proceedings are going out from here in three or four months or something of that kind, and at that time the attention of all of us will be brought back to focus, that there might well be attached to the proceedings some kind of form which would solicit from us at that time a serious recommendation. In the meantime, we might have an opportunity to discuss this with friends in other parts of the world, and here, and also to think over the matters we have discussed here. We're all a little bit terrified about coming to a quick conclusion. We don't know to what extent we are committing ourselves, and worse than that, to what extent we are committing other people. And with the two months, three months, whatever it might be, we might be prepared to sit down and do a page which is asked for in the Proceedings, and if this suggestion meets with any kind of favourable reception, I suppose there could be a motion to have this form attached to the Proceedings.

LEYERLE   I take it that is a motion, Father Shook.

SHOOK   Yes, I shall make it a motion.

COLLINS   Seconded.

LEYERLE   Seconded by Professor Collins. Would you like to discuss this motion further?

CUMMINGS   I think that I'd like to speak in favour of it, Mr Chairman, in that I feel exactly as Father Shook and as you do, Mr Chairman, in that I am appalled by any casual statement one might make here which would involve such an investment of time and talent by others, and raise their hopes when one really has to consult with others before one can do anything at all. Therefore I would like to have time to come back again to the group. This seems to me to be an exploratory meeting, and we've discovered the problems and we ought not to let it drop here. I don't know how final our actions can be unless we do constitute as a group, an ad hoc group.

LEYERLE   Further discussion?

CROSS   I feel with this too, obviously, but I wasn't intending that we should get on with a dictionary tomorrow. All I was feeling was that we should all think about it very seriously, if you like, for three months ... I support it very strongly. It wasn't my intention to rush things, but that we shouldn't go away and just let it fade away. That was all I was thinking about.

LEYERLE   Further discussion? Are you ready for the question? We can record it on the tape that we carried that unanimously.

Well, should we continue our discussion, or do you think that we have reached a point where we can proceed no further at this time?

RIGG   Could I not ask Professor Robinson again, as, in a sense, he said several times that he hopes to see an organization of some sort, if this corresponds in some way to what he would like to see?

F. ROBINSON   I gather that we have a sort of a ghost group at Toronto that perhaps will be acting as the pool, is that right? And that's the response to the thing I was suggesting. The only thing I might add is that it seems to me that it would be nice to have some formal way of keeping a representative from the people from England who are here; things like the very concrete and imaginative thinking Mr Ball has been putting into how the dictionary would go ... This kind of information will be coming in freely, it seems to me, to this Toronto group, and it would be satisfying the idea of keeping people who are practically interested and willing to contribute – sort of moving toward some concept of what it is that is wanted.

BALL   I'd like to make a gloss on that. I think it is clear from what we have decided that ongoing work in preparing editions is already in existence and will continue; and there are good committees, and they have already told us a little about their plans of finding men who will prepare these editions: this is one strand of my thinking. Another strand, of course, is the computer concordances, and it is perfectly clear that that side of things is proceeding very fast. In fact, some of us have felt, perhaps, it is going too fast, and we should stop and think of this before too many of these concordances are done. I don't suppose there will be much stopping – it is most impressive to see this work going ahead. What slightly worries me is that the dictionary itself, which I feel is the keystone of the whole project is rather lagging behind these other two; that we haven't, I think, got it clear in our minds just who is going to read what, talk to whom, write what, after today. We have this international committee, missing the vitally important North American member, and I take it that this is the group responsible for ongoing work on the dictionary itself. I would be just a little sorry, I think, if after this meeting, work proceeded on the first two strands I mentioned – the editions and the computer concordances – and the dictionary itself continued to lag behind. Now I don't see an obvious solution to this, because we haven't got the people here who have the job of going ahead with the work. We can't appoint beside them another committee to do this, but those people who are on committees, I think, should bear in mind very much the danger of allowing the dictionary itself to lie fallow, non-existent, and unplanned, for very much longer.

MITCHELL   Could I ask, on a point of information, when is it thought likely that an American representative will be appointed, or would that be a rude question? Because, in a way, he would be a man who could get in touch with Campbell and Gneuss and write directly to them; get in touch with them and see what their feelings were on the whole matter.

F. ROBINSON   I'm still having trouble with this distinction which Professor Bessinger brought up. I'm not certain what Professor Gneuss and Professor Campbell are – what they are going to do. Are they coming up with or worrying about the concrete forms that the dictionary might take and so on, and to the degree that a person would who actually anticipates moving into the work of editing slips and preparing entries themselves? Or are they a distinguished, wise, paternal group, who are overseeing things and keeping others from doing things that are too wild, but not otherwise moving? Until that's known I wouldn't be able to speculate who might emerge as an American lexicographer or how, or why ...

MITCHELL   No, I think this is it. We would have to define their positions, wouldn't we? I mean, that has become clear.

F. ROBINSON	Was it your impression from the meeting in London that Professor Gneuss and Campbell think of themselves as working editors, or not?
MITCHELL	No, I think not.
STANLEY	I think not. I think I ought to say 'wise old man' is a description difficult to accept when it comes to Professor Gneuss – who is a wise *young* man – but he is in touch with good work going on, on the Continent, just as Alistair Campbell is in touch with good work going on in England. I think it was that side of things that we had in mind in London and we certainly had the hope that there would be someone on this side of the Atlantic, though of course, our ignorance of the individuals does not allow us to produce a list of suitable names. I think we all know a good number of people whom we would think suitable for such things, but it is not for us to suggest; but that is the kind of thing we had in mind. A person who would command support and respect as we think these two do on the other side of the Atlantic. It is important that such a person be found quickly because otherwise the thinking on the dictionary is going to lag behind the other sides of this great, joint venture.
F. ROBINSON	I would only add to that, if I may, that in addition to the greatness you describe he should also rather specifically be a lexicographical person, so that thinking would be more and more concrete about the actual work that is going forward. It would be nice if this committee or the other one, if it is going to be, will be people who are involved in dictionary work.
HATCH	I haven't had much opportunity to watch the organization of scholars in something like this, so I rise with my heart in my mouth. But it seems to me on one hand that neither Professor Gneuss nor Professor Campbell wish to take on the chore of being editor: that seems to be clear from what has been said. On the other hand, there seems to be a tacit agreement among various members here that these are the men who, if not themselves the editors, are those who are going to choose the editors. Now I may be wrong about this, but it is the impression I get. If it weren't unduly pushy, perhaps I could suggest that we urge these men and whoever the American member is, and anyone else that they wish to have on their committee, to go about choosing an editor. Because it seems clear from the remarks which were made, particularly Mr Reidy's, that nothing is really going to go ahead until there is an editor who can make this kind of decision. So I throw this out, just as a possibility that this would be something we could do here and now, without unduly putting anybody on the spot about what he has to actually start doing. But it would get things going.
BESSINGER	As I understand it, the trans-Atlantic editorial committee asked Professor Campbell and Professor Gneuss to act as a dictionary committee and are still attempting to find a third person. Is that correct? I think we should get some lines of command straight here, and then ask the appropriate committees to work on it. As I understand it, based on the committees already appointed, this is the way the lines of command should work. The

trans-Atlantic editorial committee and the cis-Atlantic editorial committee together should appoint the third member of the dictionary committee, completing the panel of the troika which has been suggested. It seems to me an excellent one – two-thirds of it is excellent; I'm sure the third person will be excellent too. Then this three-member dictionary committee should convene and think hard, and brood, and pray, and appoint or approach a prospective editor. In this way, it seems to me, the slow, accumulating, ever-upward-moving authority of consensus in this group could best express itself, and we would have some sense then, I think, of due process in the formation of this very important future task. I'll make that as a motion, Mr Chairman, if it is agreeable?

LEYERLE Yes, it is.

POPE Seconded.

LEYERLE Could I ask for a point of clarification on your motion, Professor Bessinger?

BESSINGER Surely.

LEYERLE I wasn't clear – did your motion include the naming of this third party?

BESSINGER No, sir, I do not know who should be appointed as the third one, but I do understand that we have an editorial committee which was formed at the MLA in October, and ratified in December, and that this committee very appropriately then appointed a dictionary committee and asked Professors Campbell and Gneuss to serve on it, and have acceptances from these two gentlemen. Now the European and the American editorial committees should complete their job and appoint a third person, and then that three-man dictionary editorial board should proceed to find an editor. They may find the editor from among themselves, or they may go abroad.

MITCHELL You wouldn't just see it more appropriate if say some of the representatives – it was all done by people from this side of the Atlantic – the appointing of the American member. I think it would be pleasant if Professor Bessinger himself were on that committee.

BESSINGER That would be a gross violation of the principle of divided authority!

MITCHELL I think the American editorial committee would be wise to co-opt you, sir.

BESSINGER I should like to decline that very kind suggestion. Thank you. I think it would be more helpful if I stayed on the international computer board which I am going to be expanding. You may have noticed that I've been encircling people like yourself in recent weeks and getting them on to it. We may have a Laocoön-like organization here; it's going to be very snakey indeed if we are not careful.

MITCHELL No, I merely meant you as a member of that committee for the purpose of nominating the American editor, of the American editorial committee member.

BESSINGER I'll be happy to correspond informally with the committee on that subject.

LEYERLE Well, we have before us a motion which has been duly seconded. Further discussion of it?

CROSS There is a slight difficulty in that the initiative came from a meeting of a group of MLA and it seems perhaps now that you are throwing this appointment back to the European members who really have been invited in some curious way to join in the group at MLA. I would have thought that the MLA group – in the informal way that it happened in England, by consensus of opinion – perhaps could have done it without throwing the responsibility on to poor Alistair Campbell and Helmut Gneuss. Or am I being wrong in my thinking?

BESSINGER I don't think they wish to throw anything. I was not present at the meeting. I was very much in favour of what the meeting did; they chose an Englishman, a Continental, and hoped to get an American. I thought this was a very nice division of authority, and I still believe that that whole committee, not just the trans-Atlantic editorial committee, but the trans-Atlantic editorial committee plus the American one, should convene, or at least communicate and then appoint that third member of the dictionary committee. The appointment of this three-man board was the idea of the editorial committee, no one else. It was not the idea of the MLA Old English group, which has no responsibility for it.

LEYERLE I wonder, Professor Collins, if you care to speak to this since you are the one member remaining here of the editorial committee on this side.

COLLINS The editorial committee is, of course, now a great deal different from what it was at that time because now it has six English members in addition to three Americans, so it is a different group, and it will be not only a larger but a wiser group. I think that if the group wants to take on this responsibility, the opinion from across the Atlantic will be valued as well as opinions from other people here and elsewhere in the United States.

Obviously, the thing is to find someone who is really interested and willing to work and has something to say. This is the main aim, and many people may know this person, and I earnestly solicit their suggestions.

LEYERLE Further discussion? Are you ready for the question? We can again record it on tape that it was carried unanimously.

I take it then, we have done about as much as we can. Well, I would simply like to express our thanks to you all for coming and the appreciation we have for your interest and help with this conference which I hope we will all agree was a successful and enlightening one. I will simply end by picking up Professor Robinson's phrase to say that the whisky is now willing.

afterwords

The great masses of information which Professor Fred Robinson predicted would come from me as the final speaker in the Saturday afternoon session of 'Computers and Old English Concordances' never came. There just wasn't enough time. Following Professor Stanley's suggestion, I will use this 'after-word' in the Proceedings to say briefly what I would have said.

Looking back over the nine questions which I posed in the opening remarks, I can see that all of them came up at one time or another in the reports and the discussions. If there were not many firm answers, it was because the questions were large and difficult. In the sessions of the conference I was able to learn why some of them were so difficult.

The reports on computer concordances of Old English texts already in progress have convinced me that these will be of great help in the preparation of an Old English dictionary. I also realize that they can be put to a great many other linguistic and literary uses, and that it would be a mistake to shape their development to the needs of a dictionary alone.

On the dictionary itself and its preparation I have three suggestions to make. My awareness of these comes from my own experiences during research into the semantic description of a few Old English nouns, their compounds and derivatives.

The first is the need for complete and careful bibliographical preparation for a dictionary, so that no previous scholarly work is overlooked or wasted. There should be handlists of all dissertations on Old English topics, bibliographies of word studies, lexicographical and etymological notes. At centres where work on the dictionary is progressing, reference collections based on these handlists and bibliographies could be gathered. Photo-copying makes such collecting possible.

The second is the need for the fullest possible use of all textual materials available to us. Lexicographers working with more recent periods of English or with other languages often have too many texts from which to draw citations. We on the other hand have a small and well-described corpus of texts. To make a dictionary of Old English I think we should use the printed editions of these texts and all the work which has gone into them, but also, since there are microfilms and other means of making manuscript facsimiles, we should use these too. The Centre for Medieval Studies at the University of Toronto is currently making a collection of microfilms of all the manuscripts described in N. R. Ker's *Catalogue of Manuscripts containing Anglo-Saxon*. Such a collection will be of great help in supplementing a collection of printed texts for use in lexicographical work. The misunderstood suggestion about concording texts, in part, from manuscript facsimiles was not an attempt to throw out the printed editions and get back to first principles, but was intended to combine information from both printed editions and facsimiles, as both are of interest and readily available to scholars.

Some of the difficulty over printed editions and facsimiles was resolved in my mind when it became clear in the course of the conference that linguists and literary scholars meant different things by the word 'text.' To the linguist – and Professor Pillsbury stated his position – the text is what is found in the manuscript, and he is interested in describing the forms of the language, even the errors of language which are found there. To the literary scholar – Professor Clemoes stated his position – the manuscript copy is a step through which he can recover what the author actually wrote. The editors of an Old English dictionary will have to work to reconcile these different interests.

The third is the need for experimentation with a wide variety of linguistic techniques to see that the user of an Old English dictionary is presented with the maximum amount of information as clearly as possible. Mr Ball has dealt with a number of these possibilities, and I can only support what he has said. I hope that, rather than representing one 'school' of linguistic thought, an Old English dictionary will be able to borrow techniques where it sees the need.

ANGUS CAMERON, JUNE 1969

The motion made on Saturday afternoon by Professor Bessinger and seconded by Professor Pope was put into operation swiftly. Over breakfast in the Park Plaza Hotel in Toronto on Sunday morning, 23 March, those members of the European and American editorial committees still in Toronto agreed that Professor Fred C. Robinson should be the American member of the International Advisory Committee. This decision was presented to the absent members of both committees; all approved the nomination. Meanwhile, Professor Robinson had left Toronto en route to Europe for several weeks of research; he learned of his nomination some days later, but still in time to make effective use of his European trip to consult with Professors Campbell and Gneuss about appointing the editor of the dictionary.

By the end of May, the International Advisory Committee had reached a decision which is best given in the words that the Committee used to report its work:

If the Centre for Medieval Studies at the University of Toronto can be persuaded to sponsor the Old English Dictionary, then Toronto seems to us the best location for the project. The best available editors to get the dictionary underway at Toronto would seem to be Mr Angus Cameron, who is located at the Centre for Medieval Studies, and Mr C. J. E. Ball, who is now at Lincoln College, Oxford. The present committee agrees, as requested, to expand itself after consultation with the editors and to continue as an advisory committee to the editors. We are still considering, however, the question of the ultimate size of this committee, a matter which must be considered in the light of possible problems of communicating among a large number of committee members in different parts of the world, as well as of the difficulties which a large committee might have in reaching a consensus on various issues. We have discussed the question of finding a publisher for the dictionary; Professor Campbell will discuss the project with Mr D. M. Davin, Secretary to the Delegates of the Oxford Press, next month, and Professor Gneuss will sound out some German publishers. Finally, we have begun to formulate various specific suggestions on matters of procedure and policy in planning the dictionary. These will be communicated directly to the editors themselves, once they have been formally installed.

After consultation with my colleagues, I wrote on behalf of the Centre for Medieval Studies at the University of Toronto to the International Advisory Committee accepting the responsibility of sponsoring the Dictionary of Old English. The extent and limitations of this responsibility of the Centre concerning the Dictionary of Old English are stated in my letter of acceptance of 11 July 1969:

I write now to accept the invitation issued by the International Advisory Committee to the Centre for Medieval Studies to sponsor the Old English Dictionary project which will be under the editorship of Mr Angus Cameron of Toronto and Mr C. J. E. Ball of Lincoln College, Oxford. Some of the responsibilities of this sponsorship have already been met: we have adequate office space, a microfilm archive of all MSS containing Old English now in formation, storage space for some of the editorial material, and some clerical assistance. We are soliciting further financial support for responsibilities that seem likely to arise: a partial stipend for Mr Cameron so he may have time released from teaching duties to work on the dictionary; provision for research assistants; travel funds so that the editors can meet together from time to time; conference funds so that policy decisions can be reached by all those responsible for them in joint deliberation; added clerical support; provision for computer time and related soft-ware; supplies; and the like. Acceptance of this invitation involves acknowledgment of the administrative support needed and the assurance that we will work to provide it effectively and as it is needed. I also note that the formulation of policy on the dictionary itself rests with the International Advisory Committee (as it may be expanded) and the editors.

By mid-summer Mr Ball and Mr Cameron both agreed to undertake the job as joint editors of the Dictionary of Old English.

Another development was that Professor L. A. Cummings of the University of Waterloo, in Ontario, and Professor Aldo Bernardo of the State University of New York at Binghamton, reported that the computer facilities at their universities would be available to assist the project. The University of Waterloo then created an office for computer research in the Arts and Sciences and appointed Dr Philip H. Smith, Jr, as its director. The relative

proximity to Toronto of the computer facilities at Waterloo is a great convenience and cooperation has already proved to be easy and fruitful.

There seemed no possibility that the proceedings would be ready in three
or four months, as Professor Shook had hoped when he moved that a circu-
lar be sent out with the volume. Consequently, in May I sent to all those
who had attended the conference an interim report, a questionnaire, and a
copy of a detailed proposal made by Professor E. G. Stanley. This proposal
was a development of his suggestion made on Saturday afternoon that a
series of volumes in support of the Dictionary of Old English be published.
Replies from the questionnaire have been very helpful to the editors during
their initial planning of policy to be followed in compiling the Dictionary
and the materials series. While the exact structure and contents of the latter
remain to be determined, the present volume, *Computers and Old English
Concordances,* will be the first item in the series.

The editors met again in early December when Mr Ball came to the University of Toronto to talk about the Dictionary with Mr Cameron in light of
developments during the previous nine months. During this visit the editors
were able to meet with Philip H. Smith, Jr, and to visit the offices of the
Middle English Dictionary at Ann Arbor. They are drafting working papers
on policy but wish to consult with Old English specialists throughout the
world before this material is accepted as formal instructions. To achieve
this wide consultation, a second conference for the members of the various
Dictionary committees has been scheduled for the last weekend in Septem-
ber 1970 at the University of Toronto. Arrangements for this conference
are being made by the editors, who hope to have several policy papers circulated beforehand in draft form so that they may be discussed fully and
modified as necessary at the conference itself.

JOHN LEYERLE, FEBRUARY 1970

B7